ESSENTIAL
CONSTITUTIONAL
LAW

SECOND EDITION

Cavendish
Publishing
Limited

London • Sydney

ESSENTIAL
CONSTITUTIONAL
LAW

SECOND EDITION

Andrew Beale LLB MPhil PGCE MInstLEx
Principal Lecturer in Law
Swansea Law School

Cavendish
Publishing
Limited

London • Sydney

First published in Great Britain 1995 by Cavendish Publishing Limited, The Glass House, Wharton Street, London WC1X 9PX

Telephone: 071-278 8000   Facsimile: 071-278 8080

e-mail: info@cavendishpublishing.com

Visit our Home Page on http://www.cavendishpublishing.com

© Beale, A 1997

First edition 1995

Beale, Andrew

Essential Constitutional and Administrative Law – 2nd ed

1. Administrative law – Great Britain

2. Great Britain – Constitutional law

I Title

342.4'1

ISBN 1 85941 146 0

Printed and bound in Great Britain

To Helen, Matthew, Robert and Caitlin

Foreword

This book is part of the Cavendish Essential series. The books in the series are designed to provide useful revision aids for the hard-pressed student. They are not, of course, intended to be substitutes for more detailed treatises. Other textbooks in the Cavendish portfolio must supply these gaps.

The Cavendish Essential series is now in its second edition and is a well-established favourite among students.

The team of authors bring a wealth of lecturing and examining experience to the task in hand. Many of us can even recall what it was like to face law examinations!

Professor Nicholas Bourne
General Editor, Essential Series
Swansea

Summer 1997

Acknowledgments

I would like to acknowledge the untiring support of my wife, Helen, and my father who have done so much to assist me in the publication of this book.

Preface

The purpose of this book is to provide a revision aid for the undergraduate constitutional law student.

The book divides the constitutional and administrative law course into five sections and covers all the major topics associated with the subject. In each section the reader is provided with a revision checklist and guidance on the study of essential issues that figure prominently in examinations.

Where appropriate the most recent cases, legislation and academic articles are analysed to provide the reader with the most up-to-date information necessary for success in today's competitive market-place.

The law is stated as at 1 May 1997.

Andrew Beale

Contents

1 The citizen and the constitution

You should be familiar with the following areas:

- definition and classification of constitutions
- characteristics of constitutions including the rule of law, separation of powers, independence of the judiciary and parliamentary sovereignty
- sources of our constitutional law
- European Union including its history, objectives and institutions
- effect of community law on parliamentary sovereignty

Introduction

In his textbook *Constitutional & Administrative Law* (1997), Brian Thompson makes reference to our *constitutional jigsaw*. The various pieces within this jigsaw are the institutions, of various shapes and sizes, which are fitted together by the constitution to give a complete picture of government within our State. To facilitate the process of bringing these various institutional pieces together we identify three areas into which these organs of State may fit. These areas relate to the three branches of government: executive, legislature and judiciary. The function of organs within the executive branch is to formulate policies and have conduct of administration within the State. The function of organs within the legislature is to legislate and thereby translate such policies into law. The task of the judicial branch is to adjudicate in instances of dispute and thereby enforce the laws of the State.

But if this is what a constitution does, what of constitutional law? Constitutional law is the body of law which regulates the bringing together of these organs of State and identifies how they relate to each other. Its sources are both legal and non-legal, in the sense that some are capable of enforcement in a court of law whilst others, although legally recognised as being in existence, are not. The principal legal source of our constitutional law is legislation, both primary and secondary. In addition, our common law system places emphasis on judicial interpretations of the law in cases before the courts. The non-legal sources of our constitutional law include constitutional conventions, customary rules relating both to the operation of Parliament and the Royal Prerogative and the writings of learned constitutional lawyers, whose authoritative interpretations on the operation of our constitution in themselves become a part of it.

So what are the essential issues that need to be addressed when we commence our study of constitutional law?

Do we need a written constitution?

Written constitution

In the first instance we need to understand what is meant by having a written constitution. A written constitution is one contained in one or a small group of documents. To many commentators this offers the advantages of clarity, stability and enforceability over States with unwritten constitutions (ie constitutions not to be found in one or a small group of documents).

Moreover, written constitutions are more readily accepted as enjoying the advantage of a prescriptive approach. Indeed, in his article entitled, 'The Sound of Silence: Constitutional Law Without a Constitution' (1994) *Law Quarterly Review*, Sir Stephen Sedley notes that it can be claimed:

> ... in this country we have constitutional law without having a constitution, not because our constitution is unwritten but because our constitutional law, historically at least, is merely descriptive: it offers an account of how the country has come to be governed.

Whereas Sir Stephen Sedley, a High Court judge, would acknowledge that it is wrong for our legal system to find itself adjudicating in disputes between individuals and the State where the latter, 'can move its goal posts because the rules do not prescribe where the goal posts are to be located', he would see little to suggest that a written constitution provides a solution to this problem. Indeed, Sir Stephen acknowledges that a written constitution might even aggravate the problem, for legislative and administrative experience demonstrates that 'the more detail you try to prescribe, the less you find you have actually catered for'. Moreover, few commentators would disagree that no constitution can survive the movements of time without recourse to the inherent descriptive flexibility of convention and practice.

Sir John Laws notes in 'Law and Democracy' (1995) *Public Law*, that 'though our constitution is unwritten, it can and must be articulated ... the defence of the imperatives of democracy and fundamental rights cannot be assumed but must always be asserted'. The solution is to have a constitution with an, 'understood, coherent and legally under-pinned frame'. Government beyond constitutional law is tyranny. Lord Bridge noted in *X v Morgan-Grampian* (1991):

> ... the maintenance of the rule of law is in every way as important in a free society as the democratic franchise. In our society the rule of law rests upon twin foundations: the sovereignty of the Queen in Parliament in making the law and the sovereignty of the Queen's courts in interpreting and applying the law.

Dynamic and evolving constitution

To understand the dynamic and evolving nature of our constitution requires that we give recognition to the legal importance of issues of power and accountability. We should acknowledge that much of the power within our constitution presently resides with the executive. Yet common law is the 'main crucible' of our modern constitutional law and we should recognise, as did Nolan LJ in *M v Home Office* (1992), that:

> ... the proper constitutional relationship of the executive with the courts is that the courts will respect all acts of the executive within its legal province, and that the executive will respect all decisions of the courts as to what its lawful province is.

In terms of our constitutional future, we need to be fully aware of developments in Europe. In particular, we should acknowledge the immense impact that membership of the European Union has already had on our domestic law and note the blueprint for future development and enlargement outlined in the Maastricht Treaty on European Union 1992.

Characteristics of our constitution

Rule of law

One of the central characteristics of our constitution, according to Professor A V Dicey, is our adherence to the concept of the rule of law. The importance of the rule of law lies in its ability to curtail the arbitrary exercise of power via the subjection of all to legal rules which are impartially enforced. In *The Rule of Law in Britain Today* (1989) the Constitutional Reform Centre noted that:

> Dicey held it to be essential to the rule of law that public authorities should be subject to the same law as the ordinary citizen, administered in the ordinary courts, and many of the European systems of law (based on the Roman law tradition) failed the test in giving the State a special position in law.

But such a stringent definition is too narrow in that even within our common law system the State may be seen to occupy a special position. Those who are unhappy with the limitations posed by Dicey's definition offer wider definitions which centre, such as in the Declaration of Delhi 1959, upon respect for fundamental human rights. This, however, presents a problem for our constitution, for it is one of the claims of our common law system that we protect civil liberties without explicit reference to basic rights in a positive form. The late 1940s and early 1950s saw the UK committing itself to protecting human rights, formulated in positive terms, under the UN Universal Declaration of Human Rights and the European Convention on Human Rights but neither have been incorporated into our domestic law (a matter explored in greater detail in Chapter 5).

Separation of powers

The concept of the rule of law is not alone in attempting to check the potential for arbitrary government. The concept of the separation of powers also seeks to attain this purpose by segregating both the functions and personnel of the three branches of government: executive, legislature and judiciary. The idea contained within the concept of the rule of law, that legal rules be impartially administered against all, is usually taken to justify the separation of the judiciary from the other two branches of government. In the UK we seek to achieve the independence of our judiciary by offering senior judges security of tenure under the Act of Settlement 1700, so that they might dispense justice without fear or favour. But our judiciary is not wholly independent of the executive and legislature and, as the Constitutional Reform Centre points out, we have a weak judicial branch, 'perhaps the weakest in any country where the rule of law can be said to operate'.

Parliamentary sovereignty

This is because our constitution is based upon the common law rule of parliamentary sovereignty. This means that Parliament is not only competent to legislate upon any subject matter and cannot be bound by its predecessors but also once Parliament has legislated no court can pass judgment upon the validity of that legislation. Thus, unlike the constitution of the USA with its adherence to the separation of powers, we do not have a Supreme Court with the capacity to declare legislation 'unconstitutional' and therefore devoid of legal effect. Moreover the constitutional position of our judicial branch is further weakened by the near complete fusion of our executive and legislative branches. Parliament has historically been concerned with checking the power of the executive by making it accountable for its actions. However, this accountability has been eroded by the executive coming to dominate Parliament to such an extent that in 1978 the House of Commons Select Committee on Procedure concluded that:

> ... the balance of advantage between Parliament and government in the day to day working of the constitution is now weighted in favour of the government to a degree which arouses widespread anxiety and is inimical to the proper working of our parliamentary democracy.

Judicial review

It was in part a response to this change in constitutional power that judges developed the mechanism of judicial review, so as to enable individuals to challenge executive decision-making in the High Court. The growth of judicial review and administrative law in general, considered in more detail in Chapter 4, does much to illustrate both the strengths and weaknesses contained within our constitution. It demonstrates the ability within our constitution to evolve new rules and quasi-judicial remedies to cope with the interventionism of the modern State, whilst at the same time subjecting an elected administration to the whims of an unrepresentative and unaccountable judiciary. On occasion judges have shown themselves willing to clash with a powerful executive on questions of major importance, but in so doing it has exposed deep divisions within our judiciary as to the proper constitutional role of a judge.

Indeed, locating the boundary between law and politics is one of the most difficult problems confronting any democracy. In the 1995 annual lecture to the Administrative Law Bar Association Lord Irvine QC advanced the argument for judicial self-restraint in applying judicial review, 'in deference to the sovereignty of Parliament'. But as David Pannick QC noted in *The Times*, 1995:

> judges are well aware of the constitutional reality that Parliament exercises very little control over the content of primary legislation, let alone delegated legislation or administrative decisions. Nor can Parliament realistically be expected to do so, given the growth in the business of government and in the number of discretionary powers conferred. Constitutional fictions are an unpersuasive basis for seeking to encourage judges to restrain themselves when they are asked to provide remedies for the victims of injustice or unfairness.

European Union

Rees-Mogg application

An example of our judges involving themselves, via their judicial review function, in an issue of major constitutional importance can be seen in Lord Rees-Mogg's application against ratification of the Maastricht Treaty on European Union. The political sensitivity involved in the application can be seen by the warnings given against the dangers of judicial review by Lord Hailsham, a previous Lord Chancellor, and by the Speaker, who made clear that our judges should beware of interfering with the jurisdiction of the House of Commons.

The application sought to challenge ratification of the Treaty on three grounds:

- that ratification of the protocol on social policy would render the government in breach of s 6 of the European Parliamentary Elections Act 1978;
- that ratification would be altering the content of community law without parliamentary approval; and
- that ratification of title V would be transferring part of the Royal Prerogative, associated with the power to conduct foreign and security policy, to community institutions without statutory authority.

Each of these arguments were rejected by Lord Justices Auld, Lloyd and Mann with Lloyd LJ identifying the last of them as the most interesting, but weakest, of the three. Lord Rees-Mogg, a previous Editor of *The Times* and past Chairman of the Broadcasting Standards Council, declared that the dispute was the most important constitutional case for 300 years. This claim was not accepted by the judges but the application can be seen to demonstrate two important features of our constitution. First, it makes clear that Article 9 of the Bill of Rights 1689 does not operate, in the words of Professor Geoffrey Marshall, 'to prevent judicial determination of such questions as whether resolutions of either House have a particular legal effect'. In the second instance, the application demonstrates the constitutional significance of the Maastricht Treaty on European Union.

Impact on parliamentary sovereignty

The significance of membership of the European Union to our constitution law may be gauged by its impact on the concept of parliamentary sovereignty. In her article 'The Undeniable Supremacy of EC Law' (1993) *New Law Journal*, Emma Chown notes that however reluctant some may be to acknowledge it, community law takes precedence over our national domestic law. Ever since becoming a member of the European Community in 1973 the UK has been subject to Article 189 which holds regulations and directives to be binding upon all Member States. In addition, Article 5 requires that Member States agree, 'to ensure fulfilment of (their Treaty) obligations'. Examples of the supremacy of community law can be seen in *Marleasing SA v La Commercial International de Alimentacion SA* (1989), *Francovich v Italy* (1993) and the *Factortame* litigation.

Marleasing concerned the question of whether one private party could plead the provisions of a directive against another private party (known as *horizontal effect*) where the directive had not been implemented into national legislation. In this case, the European Court of Justice confirmed the doctrine of direct effect provided for an action against the defaulting Member State but not against another private party. However, the court concluded that domestic law must be interpreted in conformity with the unimplemented directive and thereby the obligation contained within the directive was placed on the private party.

Francovich further developed an individual's right by enabling an individual to sue a State for damages when the State had failed to provide rights required by a directive. The European Court of Justice upheld a right to compensation providing there was an attribution of rights to individuals under the directive, that the content of those rights were identifiable and that there was causality between the Member State's violation of its obligation and the damage suffered by the individuals concerned.

These cases, however, involved Member States other than the UK with its constitution based on parliamentary sovereignty. Yet even in the early 1970s our judges were quick to recognise the legal impact of the European Communities Act 1972 on domestic issues with a *European element*. In *Bulmer v Bollinger SA* (1974) Lord Denning talked of a new source to our law, 'like an incoming tide. It flows into the estuaries and up the rivers. It cannot be held back'. A few years later, in *Macarthys v Smith* (1980) Lord Denning asserted that this new source:

> ... is now part of our law; and, whenever there is any inconsistency, (it) has priority. It is not supplanting English law. It is part of our law which overrides any other part which is inconsistent with it.

This position was reaffirmed in the test case of *Garland v BREL* (1983). But it was not until the *Factortame* litigation that the true impact on parliamentary sovereignty became apparent.

Factortame was a company of mostly Spanish directors and shareholders which owned and operated 95 fishing vessels from the UK. Although previously registered under the Merchant Shipping Act 1894 the vessels were no longer capable of registration under the stringent Merchant Shipping (Registration of Fishing Vessels) Regulations made under the new Merchant Shipping Act 1988. In particular the new regulations required the whole of the legal title and at least 75% of beneficial ownership to be vested in UK citizens (ie domiciled in the UK) or UK companies (ie principal place of business in the UK). The company applied for a judicial review to challenge the validity of the regulations and a *preliminary ruling* from the European Court of Justice was sought under Article 177. Pending the ruling and by way of interim relief, judges in the Divisional Court disapplied the new regulations. The Secretary of State appealed and judges in the Court of Appeal set aside the order for interim relief – a decision upheld by judges in the House of Lords. However, the judges in the House of Lords also sought a *preliminary ruling* on the granting of interim relief.

In the meantime the Commission brought an action against the UK for a declaration that the nationality provisions contained within the new regulations were in breach of the Articles 52 and 221 of the *Treaty of Rome*. The European Court of Justice held that the aim of the common fisheries policy did not warrant the new regulations, which the UK were obliged to amend by Order in Council in 1989. On the issue of the request for a *preliminary ruling* from the House of Lords, the European Court of Justice ruled that a court which would have granted interim relief but for a rule of domestic law should set aside that rule of domestic law in favour of observing Treaty obligations. Thus on matters involving a *European element* a duly passed Act of Parliament may now be effectively set aside by a UK court if it considers that the statute may violate community law. The European Court of Justice subsequently ruled that the company was entitled to compensation from the British government for the infringement of rights under Community law.

Judges in the Court of Appeal recently had an opportunity to look at the effect of the *Factortame* litigation in *R v HM Treasury, ex p British Telecom* (1993). A distinction was clearly drawn between disapplying primary and secondary legislation by the granting of an interim injunction and the judges declared that they would be far more circumspect in relation to primary legislation. Nevertheless, *Factortame* and other decisions we have cited have led judges, such as *Hoffmann* J in *Stoke-on-Trent CC v B & Q* (1991), to conclude that our Treaty obligations to the European Union are, 'the supreme law of this country, taking precedence over Acts of Parliament'. Parliamentary sovereignty may be sustained by our undoubted (though largely theoretical) right to withdraw from the European Union. However, subject to the unlikely repeal of the European Communities (Amendment) Act 1993, constitutional law students are well advised to direct their energies to understanding the Maastricht Treaty on European Union.

Journey to Maastricht

However, before we consider the Treaty in more detail we should first address our attention to the significant developments which have occurred on the road to European Union.

In 1948 the Organisation for Economic Co-operation and Development (OECD) was established with financial assistance from the USA in order to regenerate the economies of Europe after the Second World War. This was followed in 1949 with the creation of the North Atlantic Treaty Organisation or NATO (a military alliance between Europe and the USA and Canada) and the Council of Europe, from which we now have the European Convention on Human Rights (ECHR).

Led by Robert Schuman, the French Foreign Minister, 1956 saw the creation of the European Coal and Steel Community (ECSC) under the Treaty of Paris, a supra-national organisation which co-ordinated the production of coal and steel (the raw materials of war). In 1957, Germany, France, Italy, Belgium, Netherlands and Luxembourg joined together to form a European Economic Community to promote closer economic co-operation and a unified trading area. An additional Treaty of Rome signed in 1957 saw the creation of the European Atomic Energy Community (EURATOM), providing for a supra-national regulation of the non-military use of atomic energy.

The four institutions of the ECSC were the High Authority, Council, Assembly and Court of Justice. The latter two, Assembly and Court of Justice, were shared with EURATOM and the EEC and in the Merger Treaty of 1965 a Common Council and Commission of the European Communities were created for the ECSC, EURATOM and EEC (in addition to the already shared Assembly and Court of Justice).

Subsequent years have seen a growth in the size of membership of the Communities, with the UK, Denmark and Eire joining in 1972, Greece in 1981, Spain and Portugal in 1985 and Finland, Sweden and Austria in 1995.

The concept of a unified common trading market, visualised in the Treaty of Rome 1957, was realised under the Single European Act 1986. In February 1992, the Maastricht Treaty on European Union was signed, coming into force in this country in November of the following year. The Treaty consists of three pillars. The first pillar amends the EEC Treaty, making it the EC Treaty. The second pillar provides a series of statements of intent on a common foreign and security policy. The third pillar provides for a common policy on justice and home affairs.

The Maastricht Treaty therefore creates a European Union which is larger than just the European Community. But whereas decision-making in pillars two and three is achieved through inter-governmental co-operation and co-ordination, the first pillar is regulated by the institutions of the Community. These Community Institutions are the Council of Ministers, the European Commission, the Parliament and the European Court of Justice. However, all three pillars are headed by the European Council under which Heads of Government and Foreign Ministers meet twice a year to formulate major policy decisions.

We should note, therefore, that laws of the European Community, as regulated by the European Court of Justice (ECJ), only apply to the first pillar of the Union (other than where the Council determines otherwise). Nevertheless, knowledge of Community law is vital for the constitutional law student. One of the most significant legal developments introduced by the Maastricht Treaty on European Union has been the concept of subsidiarity.

Subsidiarity

Article 3b

Article 3b of the Maastricht Treaty on European Union provides that:

> The community shall act within the limits of the powers conferred upon it by this Treaty and of the objectives assigned to it therein. In areas which do not fall within its exclusive competence, the community shall take action, in accordance with the principle of subsidiarity, only if and in so far as the objectives of the proposed action cannot be sufficiently achieved by the Member States and can therefore, by reason of the scale or effects of the proposed action, be better achieved by the community.
>
> Any action by the community shall not go beyond what is necessary to achieve the objectives of this Treaty.

Although attention has tended to focus exclusively on the principle of subsidiarity it should be recognised that Article 3b contains two other distinct, though complementary, concepts. These three principles are together designed to provide a constitutional foundation upon which European Union can be further developed. The principle of the attribution of powers simply means that the community is only entitled to act where given the express power to do so. Clearly, the implementation of this principle requires an assessment of whether the proposed action falls within the limits of the powers conferred by the Treaty and is aimed at meeting one or more of its objectives.

The above principle, requiring the community to justify its ability to act, is supplemented by the key concept of subsidiarity. According to this principle, as it may be understood in its strict legal sense, the community not only has to justify its ability to act, but also justify why it and not the Member States should act. This will, of course, necessitate an evaluation of whether the objectives of the proposed action can be sufficiently achieved by the action of Member States and if not, can they, therefore, be better achieved by action on the part of the community.

There is, however, an important qualification on the operation of the principle of subsidiarity, namely, that it cannot be applied to matters falling within the community's exclusive competence, sometimes referred to as the *occupied field*. In short, the principle of subsidiarity,

11

despite all the attention paid to it, is only intended to operate in relation to those areas where the community has a parallel competence with Member States. The issue of differing competences was addressed by the Foreign Secretary in a Commons debate in July 1992. Douglas Hurd argued that policies today fall into one of three categories:

- where the community has no competence;
- where the community has exclusive competence; and
- where the community has a parallel competence with Member States.

It was at the personal instigation of Douglas Hurd that the third principle, that of proportionality or intensity, was applied not only to areas of parallel competence, but also to areas of exclusive competence. This clearly gives proportionality greater potential than subsidiarity for acting as a rule of minimum interference. The principle itself requires that the intensity of community action must always be in proportion to the objective being pursued.

2 The citizen and the legislature

You should be familiar with the following areas:

- House of Lords including composition, functions, reform or abolition
- House of Commons including composition and functions
- Nolan Committee
- Ombudsfolk
- parliamentary privilege

Introduction

In Chapter 1 we noted the importance of the concept of parliamentary sovereignty. In this chapter we will study the role performed by Parliament and in so doing recognise that the *Queen in Parliament* is the supreme law-making power within our State.

Parliament is bicameral, in that it consists of two legislative chambers. The House of Lords is still referred to today as the *Upper* House. At one time this accurately reflected its significance in relation to the other chamber, the House of Commons. In an agriculturally based society, land is the primary factor of production. The feudal system, introduced into our State in Norman times, ensured that the great landowners were the nobility. Even today members of our nobility still sit by hereditary right in the House of Lords.

But the continuing growth in democracy within our State led to the *Lower Chamber*, as the only elected chamber, acquiring increasing significance until, at the beginning of this century, it successfully challenged the *Upper* House for constitutional supremacy.

Establishing legislative supremacy is, however, distinct from saying that Parliament 'runs the country'. Even in the last century Prime Minister Gladstone made clear that it was not the role of Parliament to govern the country, but to call to account those who do govern the country. It is now our task to analyse the success of methods employed by Parliament to achieve this aim.

Accountability via debate

Ministerial responsibility

We have seen in Chapter 1 that the concept of parliamentary sovereignty demands that Parliament has no legislative rival. The supremacy of Parliament in making law needs to be considered, however, within the context of the convention of ministerial responsibility (considered in more detail in Chapter 3).

This important convention of our constitution recognises that far from separating the personnel within our executive from the legislature, our constitution requires, with the notable exception of the civil service, that members of our executive are drawn exclusively from the legislature. This overlap between the two branches is regarded by some as essential to the efficient operation of our constitution. This is because the convention demands that the legislative programme of the government of the day must command the confidence of the legislature, without which the government is collectively obliged to resign. It is logical, therefore, for convention to require also that the Monarch appoint as Prime Minister a person able to command a majority in Parliament.

On the face of it this would seem to demonstrate considerable power on the part of our Parliament within the constitution. The very survival of the government turns on the day-to-day support for its legislative programme. But this very fact has led to developments within our constitution which counter-balance the inherent instability this poses.

Power of the House of Lords

In the first instance, we should recognise that limitations have now been placed upon the power of the House of Lords to call the government to account for its legislative proposals. In 1909 the House of Lords sought to use its powers under the constitution to reject the Finance Bill (Budget) proposed by the Liberal government. The duly elected government of the day objected to this exercise of veto by the unelected chamber and sought the advice of the Monarch as 'constitutional referee'. King George V suggested that the people be left to decide the issue and after two general elections in 1910, and the threat of the King to create enough Liberal (hereditary) peers to get the measure through, the House of Lords accepted the Parliament Act 1911.

Under this Act government Bills could be enacted without the consent of the House of Lords which now only had a power to delay legislation for three successive sessions (two years). This delaying power was reduced, under the Parliament Act 1949 to two successive sessions (one year). Moreover, Bills certified as 'Money Bills' by the Speaker could attain Royal assent direct from the House of Commons, if they had been placed before the House of Lords for a minimum period of a month.

In recognition of the legislative supremacy of the elected chamber these procedures have been used on only four occasions – to pass the Welsh Church Act 1914, Government of Ireland Act 1914, Parliament Act 1949 and War Crimes Act 1991. This is not to say, however, that the House of Lords is not capable of inflicting embarrassing defeats and amendments to government proposals.

Party system

In the second instance, we should also recognise that much has happened within the House of Commons to ensure that the government of the day can count upon its legislative support. With the growth in enfranchisement and universal adult suffrage came the corresponding growth in political parties. Originating as a loose association of like-minded individuals elected to office, these political parties soon developed an infrastructure and 'whip system'. The purpose of the 'whip system' was and still is to maximise party effect by ensuring a disciplined collective vote on legislative matters.

One might consider that it is not unreasonable for a government comprised of Ministers drawn exclusively from members of one political party, predominantly within the House of Commons, to expect the support of colleagues committed to implementing the same election manifesto. Nevertheless, there has been criticism that the demands of party loyalty have done much to undermine the 'individuality' of our elected representatives, who, far from calling the executive to account for their legislative proposals, may be seen to act as mere 'lobby fodder' for the party machine they serve.

Public Bills

It may be argued that Members of Parliament do have a role to play in initiating debate within Parliament on matters of national or constituency interest. Standing Orders provide an opportunity for a

Member of Parliament to initiate an emergency debate on an important matter that requires urgent consideration. The Ten Minute Rule provides an opportunity for backbench Members of Parliament to speak in favour of legislative debate on a proposed Bill. In addition, members might also sponsor a Public Bill as their own Private Members Bill. At the end of the day's business, members may initiate an adjournment debate on local or personal issues. Such opportunities are, however, very limited with little realistic chance of success unless the MP has government support for the proposal. Parliamentary time is at a premium and it is the task of the Leader of the House to ensure that such time as is available is maximised to ensure the smooth passage of the government's legislative programme for the parliamentary session. To this end the government has considerable procedural powers at its disposal including the *guillotine*, under which time for debate at one or more stages of a Bill can be restricted.

Legislative stages

The various legislative stages undertaken by government Bills on matters of public importance include:

- first reading (formal introduction of the proposal);
- second reading (where the principles of the Bill are considered and a vote taken);
- committee stage (where a standing committee scrutinises the Bill in detail);
- report stage (where the chair of the standing committee reports to the House on the committee's deliberations); and
- the third reading and vote which complete the Bill's passage through the House of Commons and denotes its progression to 'the other place'.

Although procedures do vary, the stages in the House of Lords are much the same. Once the Bill has received a third reading in the House of Lords it is presented for Royal assent which, by convention, should not be withheld. These legislative procedures have been criticised by Howard Davies, then Director-General of the Confederation of British Industry, as providing insufficient opportunity for consultation. Speaking to the European Policy Forum in March 1994 he argued that greater consultation would avoid, 'bad law and expensive ambiguities which have to be resolved in the courts'.

Different parliamentary stages, however, apply to Private Bills which are promoted by individuals or bodies to give powers in addition to or varying from the general law and Hybrid Bills (in essence a Public Bill specifically affecting an individual's private rights).

Delegated legislation

But whereas the principle of the legislation is often contained within a statute, much of the fine detail of its law will be enacted through delegated legislation. There are different types of delegated legislation to which different levels of parliamentary scrutiny apply.

An interesting development in this regard has been the creation of a Select Committee on the Scrutiny of Delegated Power for the House of Lords. When recommending its creation the Procedure Committee noted, 'democracy is not only about the election of politicians, but about setting limits to their powers'.

Under Standing Order 101, the House of Commons will also have one or more Standing Committees for the consideration of delegated legislation with effect from the session 1996–97.

The most common types of delegated or subordinate legislation are Statutory Instruments (see Statutory Instruments Act 1946) and Orders in Council. It is important to note that many of the directives referred to in Chapter 1 are implemented into our law via delegated legislation, to which a special form of parliamentary review procedure applies. In this and all other areas of delegated legislation the Parliament Acts 1911 and 1949 do not apply, thus giving the House of Lords the same power of veto as the House of Commons.

Accountability via questioning and investigation

Questions

One of the more visible demonstrations of a Minister's accountability to Parliament is the practice of requiring Ministers to come to Parliament on a regular basis to answer oral questions from backbench Members of Parliament on the operation of their respective departments.

This demonstration of our parliamentary democracy in action may provide an interesting spectacle for the recent broadcasting of proceedings but the practice is of limited value in calling the executive to account for its action. The Prime Minister is required to attend for questions, during which time the Speaker will permit the Leader of the Opposition supplementary questions. The purpose of the exercise, however, has become one of point scoring between these political adversaries and providing an appropriate 'sound-bite' for subsequent media use. In addition to oral questions backbench Members of Parliament may also, and more usually pose, written questions to Ministers often relating to a constituent's grievance.

Departmental select committees

In recognition of the limited effectiveness of parliamentary scrutiny by questioning the all party Select Committee on Procedure recommended in 1978 that a new system of departmental select committees be introduced to scrutinise the 'policy, administration and finance' of departments of State. When introducing this reform soon after the general election in 1979 the Leader of the House, Norman St John-Stevas (now Lord St John-Stevas), announced to the House of Commons that, 'after years of discussion and debate, we are embarking upon a series of changes that could constitute the most important parliamentary reforms of the century'.

Inquiry into the 'Supergun Affair'

There were, therefore, high hopes in 1979 that this new system of investigative committees would do much to redress the balance of power between Parliament and the executive to enable the House of Commons to do more effectively the job it had been elected to do. But to what extent has this potential been realised today?

A case study in the present day effectiveness of a departmental select committee investigation is provided by the inquiry of the Trade and Industry Select Committee into the 'Supergun Affair'.

In his article, 'Matrix Churchill, 'Supergun and the Scott Inquiry' *Public Law* (1993) Ian Leigh notes, 'in retrospect it seems clear that the Committee were seriously misled in their conclusions'. Sir Hal Miller, whose initial allegations had prompted the select committee inquiry refused to testify. Given that he was a Member of Parliament his attendance could only be compelled by a House of Commons resolution, which was not attempted by the Committee, 'because it was felt that a motion of this kind would be defeated by the government'.

The Committee were denied access to some potential witnesses. No direct access was permitted, for example, to members of the intelligence services with knowledge of the supergun project. Some civil servants, such as Eric Beston from the Department of Trade and Industry, were forbidden by Ministers from testifying (when others, such as

Mark Higson from the Foreign Office, did testify, they exposed the inadequacy of parliamentary questioning by detailing the drafting of misleading replies used by Ministers).

Moreover, Ian Leigh noted the effect of party political pressures on the Committee's work, which were heightened because of the proximity of a general election. He concluded that:

> ... despite the obvious appeal of select committees from the standpoint of the democratic ideal ... (there) are serious objections to the role of select committees reviewing executive action with intelligence implications .... If Parliament allows itself to be deterred from increased intelligence scrutiny and a more probing role for select committees generally, it will only have itself to blame.

The 1800 page report by Sir Richard Scott, *The Report of the Inquiry into the Export of Defence Equipment and Dual-Use Goods to Iraq and related Prosecutions* (HE 115), published on 15 February 1996, made a number of important findings, not least of which were that Parliament had been 'deliberately' misled by government Ministers, and that the Matrix Churchill trial 'ought never to have commenced'. However, the Report also concluded that the government had no intention of sending innocent men to jail by blocking the release of crucial documents during the trial.

When asked to comment on Sir Robin Butler's (Head of the Civil Service) evidence to the Scott Inquiry that it was possible for Ministers to give Parliament 'an accurate but incomplete answer', William Waldegrave, as the Member responsible for open government, informed the Treasury and Civil Service Select Committee that, 'much of government activity is ... like playing poker. You do not put all your cards up at one time'. Mr Waldegrave then asserted that Ministers could find that, 'in exceptional cases (such as an impending currency devaluation), it is necessary to say something that is untrue to the House of Commons'.

In his report, Sir Richard Scott stated that:

> the withholding of information by an accountable minister should never be based on reasons of convenience or for the avoidance of political embarrassment, but should always require special and carefully considered justification ... the proposition that it is acceptable for a Minister to give an answer that is deliberately incomplete is one which, in my opinion, is inconsistent with the requirements of the constitutional principle of ministerial accountability.

It is interesting to note that John Profumo, the disgraced War Minister, was not forced to resign in 1963 because of his private life but because he had lied about it to the House of Commons.

Nevertheless, in his assessment of the Scott Report, Professor Vernon Bogdanor argues that, 'perhaps the deepest lesson of the Scott Inquiry is that Parliament is in danger of losing its capacity to bring Ministers to account'. This concern is echoed by Professor Dawn Oliver who would note that through its consideration of the Report's findings, 'Parliament resat an old exam in the Arms to Iraq affair, and failed yet again'.

Accountability via scrutiny of national finance

Parliament's role

Our system of national finance may be viewed as amounting to little more than, 'the Crown demands money, the Commons grants it and the Lords assents to the grant'. Others might argue, however, that in running our nation's finances the executive remains effectively accountable to Parliament in two important respects. In the first instance only Parliament has the legal authority to sanction public expenditure and revenue. Secondly, it is the ultimate responsibility of Parliament to ensure that any expenditure which has been sanctioned is both properly and efficiently spent. It is our task to assess the extent to which these mechanisms provide an adequate opportunity for Parliament to call the executive to account for its control of national finance.

Public expenditure

In terms of spending, public expenditure takes the two forms of consolidated fund services and supply services. Consolidated fund services relate to charges on the 'public revenue' or 'public funds' under 'Permanent Acts' which give a continuing authority to pay for these services out of the Consolidated Fund or National Loans Fund. Supply services relate to charges paid out of 'money provided by Parliament' which require a specific statutory authority to pay for the service out of the Consolidated Fund or National Loans Fund.

Public revenue

In terms of raising money to pay for national expenditure, some revenue is derived from Crown land (which is given to the State in return for the Civil List) but the vast majority is raised through the imposition of taxes. Some taxation is authorised by Parliament in the form of

'Permanent Acts', which remain in force until repealed or amended, eg VAT. Other taxes such as Income Tax and Customs and Excise Duty are, however, authorised by 'Annual Acts' which remain in force for a year and as, 'charges upon the people' are part of 'ways and means business'.

Parliamentary scrutiny

Whereas it must be said that parliamentary support for the government's proposals on expenditure and taxation will divide along party lines, the same cannot be said of parliamentary scrutiny of how the executive spends public money. The National Audit Act 1983 had as its purpose the strengthening of parliamentary supervision over expenditure by providing for a National Audit Office, headed by a Comptroller and Auditor General, and the establishment of a Public Accounts Commission. The intention is that these bodies should work with the Public Accounts Committee of the House of Commons to promote economy, efficiency and effectiveness in the use of public money.

Public Accounts Committee

It is interesting to note in this context, therefore, that in late January 1994 the all party Public Accounts Committee produced an unprecedented Report criticising the growth in waste and corruption within the public sector. The Committee stated in its report:

> ... in recent years we have seen and reported on a number of serious failures in administrative and financial systems and controls within departments and other public bodies, which have led to money being wasted or otherwise improperly spent ... these failings represent a departure from the standards of public conduct which have mainly been established during the last 140 years (The Northcote-Trevelyan Report having exposed nepotism and incompetence in our civil service 140 years ago).

The worst examples of waste included £56.6m lost by the Property Services Agency when its invoicing system broke down, £55m in 'doubtful and incorrect payments' by the Department of Employment, £20m lost by the Wessex Regional Health Authority on a failed computer system and £10m lost by the West Midlands Health Authority as part of a privatisation programme. Highlighting growing signs of fraud and corruption, the Committee criticised the Foreign Office for inadequate accounting controls in 1989 which created a 'climate conducive to fraud and theft' and the Welsh Development Agency which, in addition to giving a Director a retirement package of £228,000 after eight months 'gardening leave', employed a 'crook' to run the international side of its operation after he supplied a fictitious reference alleged to have come from a Home Office Minister.

The importance of this investigation into the present lack of financial responsibility shown by government departments and the 1,444 quangos and health trusts (see Chapter 4) now running public services is not to be underestimated. It is a telling statistic that in Wales these otherwise unaccountable quangos now spend £2.1 billion from the public purse, almost the equivalent of all local government expenditure within the Principality. Moreover, the First Steps Initiative (outlined in Chapter 3) ensures that this level of expenditure will continue to increase.

Parliamentary privilege

Freedom of speech

Parliamentary privilege is part of the law and custom of Parliament. We are informed by Erskine May that it is a necessary requirement of our constitution for without it Members of Parliament, 'could not discharge their functions'. The most important privilege is that of freedom of speech and debate. Article 9 of the Bill of Rights 1689 provides that:

> ... freedom of speech and debates or proceedings in Parliament ought not to be impeached or questioned in any court or place out of Parliament.

The issue of what is covered by the term 'proceedings in Parliament' was raised in the case of *G R Strauss* (1958). George Strauss MP sought to use parliamentary privilege to protect himself from a threat by the London Electricity Board to sue him for defamation, resulting from the Paymaster General passing on to the Board his letter complaining about the way in which they disposed of scrap cable. The Committee of Privileges felt that the Board had been in breach of Article 9 but it was not a view shared by the chamber as a whole. However, even if communications between Members and Ministers are not covered by Parliamentary privilege it is clear that, as with letters from members of the public to Members of Parliament, such communications are protected by qualified privilege. Qualified privilege offers a defence to a defamation action, providing the communication is not made maliciously or spitefully.

Other privileges

Other privileges enjoyed by Members of Parliament include their collective right to regulate both the chamber's composition and proceedings. Whereas the determination of election petitions have now been transferred to an election court presided over by judges, the case of *Gary Allighan* (1947) clearly demonstrates a power to expel a duly elected member from the chamber. In addition, the cases of *Bradlaugh v Gossett* (1884) and *R v Graham-Campbell, ex p Herbert* (1935) can also be used to demonstrate judicial acceptance of the notion that members have a right to claim exclusive cognisance over all internal matters.

Courts and parliamentary privilege

In the past Parliament has always claimed to be the sole and absolute judge of its own privileges. Evidence for this can be seen in the case of *Stockdale v Hansard* (1839) and the related *Case of the Sheriff of Middlesex* (1840). Difficulties arose here because the courts maintained a right to determine the nature and limit of parliamentary privilege where it affected the rights of individuals outside Parliament. Whereas this matter had to be settled eventually by the passing of the Parliamentary Papers Act 1840, an interesting development in this area can be seen in the case of *Rost v Edwards* (1990). In this case Popplewell J stated that where there is uncertainty as to whether Parliament or the courts have jurisdiction over an issue of parliamentary privilege the courts should, 'not be astute to find a reason for ousting the jurisdiction of the court and for limiting or even defeating a proper claim by a party to litigation before it'.

The case of *Allason v Haines* (1995) illustrated difficulties which were occurring in the courts, resultant from parliamentary privilege, in litigation involving Members of Parliament. Following the decision of the Privy Council in *Prebble v Television New Zealand* (1994), Owen J was content to stay the libel action bought by the Member of Parliament, on the grounds that parliamentary privilege prevented the defendants putting forward the defence they wished to put forward.

Further difficulties were experienced by Neil Hamilton and Ian Greer Associates when their defamation action against the *Guardian* newspaper was also stayed. Despite warnings from Lord Simon that, 'it is nearly impossible to exaggerate the constitutional importance of ... changes to parliamentary privilege' changes were in consequence made to the effect of Article 9 of the Bill of Rights 1689. Where the conduct of a person in, or in relation to proceedings in, Parliament is an issue in defamation proceedings, those proceedings can now be questioned in court under s 13 of the Defamation Act 1996. Nevertheless, there can be no liability for words spoken or things done in the course of any proceedings in Parliament and this exception to Article 9 of the Bill of Rights only applies to issues of defamation.

Contempt

But whereas both the Courts and Parliament may on occasion claim a jurisdiction to adjudicate on issues of parliamentary privilege, Parliament will always claim an ultimate power to punish breaches of parliamentary privilege for contempt of the House. It is interesting to note, however, that in performing this judicial type function the House acts as victim, prosecutor and judge. It has already been held, in a case involving the Maltese legislature, that such an adjudication contravenes Article 6 of the European Convention on Human Rights. Furthermore, it should be noted that an individual against whom a Member of Parliament has made a complaint for breach of parliamentary privilege is not entitled to be heard, legally represented, call evidence or cross-examine witnesses.

Privileges of peers

Whereas emphasis is not unnaturally given to the privileges enjoyed by Members of Parliament it should not be forgotten that parliamentary privilege also extends to the other chamber in the legislature. Despite its recommended abolition by the Committee on Parliamentary Privilege in 1967, members of the House of Lords like their legislative colleagues in the House of Commons still enjoy freedom from civil arrest. Moreover, they also have rights relating to the regulation of their chamber.

The Nolan Committee on Standards of Conduct in Public Life

In its Report on the 'Sunday Times cash for questions affair' the Committee of Privileges found that the conduct of members who tabled parliamentary questions in return for payment 'fell short of the standards' expected by the House. Of the two members involved, one was formally reprimanded and suspended for 20 days without pay and the other was reprimanded and suspended for 10 days. In response to this and a general concern about 'sleaze' in public life, the Committee on Standards in Public Life was established in 1994 to act, in the words of Prime Minister John Major, as 'an ethical workshop' providing 'running repairs on standards in public life'.

The Committee's first report, published in 1995, made important recommendations for the reform of Parliament. In particular, it was proposed that the rules on disclosure of Members' interests should be tightened up and regulated by a new Parliamentary Commissioner for Standards (Sir Gordon Downey appointed in November 1995), working with a new Select Committee for Privileges and Standards. Members are now prohibited from entering into paid advocacy agreements on behalf of private companies. The Leader of the House, noted that 'these are undoubtedly the most significant changes in the rules relating to the House of Commons since the introduction of the Register of Members' Interests in 1974'. Responding to the investigations of its own Griffiths Committee, the House of Lords has also agreed to a register of financial interests and for Peers not to sell their parliamentary influence.

Given its status as a standing committee, it still remains to be seen whether the Nolan Committee can live up to Professor Peter Hennessy's billing as, 'a miniature, if informal, constitutional convention'. Nevertheless, the fact that it is a catalyst for constitutional reform is beyond doubt. For example, the Royal Commission on Standards of Conduct in Public Life, 1976, chaired by Lord Salmon, recommended the rationalisation of the law on bribery and corruption in public life. The Nolan Committee pointed out that whilst the government had accepted this recommendation, it had failed to implement it and invited the Law Commission to take this reform forward. The Law Commission, chaired by Dame Mary Arden, a High Court judge, have accepted this invitation and would now propose a single offence of corruption. This coincides with the Home Office proposing clarification of the laws on bribery of Members of Parliament. One option would be to extend the present law, so that it includes Members of Parliament. This proposal would be controversial, however, because it would extend the jurisdiction of the courts over Members of Parliament.

Parliamentary Commissioner for Administration

'Grievance man'

In order to facilitate the work of backbench Members of Parliament the government of the day in 1967 acceded to a proposal contained within the Whyatt Report 1962 to create the office of the Parliamentary Commissioner for Administration, perhaps better known as the Ombudsman (Scandinavian for 'grievance man'). In introducing what was to become the Parliamentary Commissioner for Administration Act 1967 the relevant Minister, Richard Crossman, welcomed the introduction of an official who was intended to provide 'a cutting-edge' for Members of Parliament investigating maladministration within the executive branch of State.

Ombudsfolk

The creation of this 'grievance man' heralded the start of the growth in various Ombudspeople. In addition to giving the Parliamentary Commissioner the dual function of looking at administration within the Health Service, new Ombudspeople were created for local government (first in Northern Ireland then for England and Wales and finally Scotland). New Ombudspeople continue to be created. Under the Courts and Legal Services Act 1990 a Legal Services Ombudsperson was created and we have already noted the creation of a Parliamentary Committee for Standards. Moreover these statutory ombudspeople have been joined by a growing band of colleagues supervising the private sector.

'Cutting edge'?

The creation of the office of the Parliamentary Commissioner for Administration (PCA) may have been the catalyst for these developments but the question can be posed, to what extent has this original office fulfilled its intended purpose? In their article, 'A "Cutting Edge"? The Parliamentary Commissioner and Members of Parliament' *Modern Law Review* (1990) Professor Gavin Drewry and Professor Carol Harlow concluded that:

> Crossman's description of the Parliamentary Commissioner as the 'cutting-edge' of the backbenchers' complaints service looks today like empty rhetoric.

Of the representative sample of Members of Parliament interviewed, 67% described the office as being of only slight value to them and 11% believed it to be of no value to them whatsoever. The research revealed that, 'for too many Members of Parliament the (PCA) ... has no *raison d'être'*, and that together with their staff they relate more to the civil servants whose work they are called upon to investigate than Members of Parliament whose servants they ultimately are.

Twenty-five year review

More recently when William Reid, the present Parliamentary Commissioner, issued his Report for 1991 Professor Anthony Bradley took the opportunity to review the office in its 25 years of operation. In his article entitled, 'Sachsenhausen, Barlow Clowes – and then?' *Public Law* (1992) Professor Bradley noted the aforementioned successes and the fact that when complaints are investigated 90% are found to be either fully or partly justified (as compared to 10% in 1967) but concluded that Professor Griffith's prediction of an office erring on the side of caution and insulated from complainants has proved to be all too true.

Citizen's charter

It may be thought that the services provided by the PCA would form an important part in the government's Citizen's Charter: Raising the Standard 1991. The work of the PCA in fact receives scant attention and emphasis has instead been given to a system of 'Lay Adjudicators'. The first of these, Elizabeth Filkin, took up office in July 1993 as the Revenue Adjudicator. In an article, 'A New Breed of Ombudsperson?' *Public Law* (1993) Professor Dawn Oliver notes that, '... the Adjudicator, unlike the Parliamentary Commissioner for Administration, is not directly accountable to the House of Commons and has no direct link with the House'. Professor Oliver concludes that this appointment therefore represents, 'an interesting departure from the traditional monopoly of "redress of grievance" functions by the Commons'.

The future

More recently, the Select Committee on the Parliamentary Commissioner for Administration has undertaken a far-reaching inquiry into the powers, work and jurisdiction of the Ombudsman.

The vast majority of the recommendations made by the Committee, as a result of its review, have been accepted by the government. This 1993 review may therefore be seen to represent an important step in the development of an office which, in the view of Professor Anthony Bradley, is already making 'a positive and original contribution to the improvement of public administration'.

Evidence for this can be seen in the Ombudsman's investigation of maladministration in the Channel Tunnel Rail Link development. Whereas the Department of Transport had refused to accept that there had been any maladministration, the government did agree to compensate individuals who had been the subject of 'blight', 'out of respect for the PCA Select Committee and the Office of the Parliamentary Commissioner'.

The accountability of Parliament

Unelected chamber

So far we have concentrated upon the constitutional accountability *to* Parliament, but what of the accountability *of* our Parliament? In States which claim to be representative democracies the usual constitutional mechanism employed to ensure accountability to the public is that of elections. Yet we have already noted that one of our parliamentary chambers, the House of Lords, is unelected. Thus under our constitution we have a government, predominantly from the elected chamber, which is made accountable for its actions to an unaccountable chamber. We have already noted that this ultimately led to the removal of the chamber's legislative power of veto over primary legislation. But this is not to say that the 'Upper' House is not without power or significance today.

Some would argue that this power and influence stems from the fact that members of the chamber do not have an electorate to please. This, combined with a less domineering party whip system, ensures a greater degree of independence amongst its members who are perhaps more readily able to view things in terms of the national interest than their elected colleagues, who are obliged to take constituency and party interests into account. The composition of the House of Lords may, therefore, be seen both as its weakness and its strength.

It is important to note, however, that the composition of the House of Lords has undergone important and comparatively recent change. The House of Lords today is still composed of Lords Spiritual, in recognition of our State religion, and Lords Temporal. The latter, which includes hereditary peers and the 'Law lords', had a new category of peer added to it with the Life Peerages Act 1958. These new life peers may only be numerically half the size of hereditary peers but, being amongst the most active of members, their impact on the work of the chamber has been significant. Another reform introduced in 1958 was to allow disinterested hereditary peers the opportunity to apply for a leave of absence from the chamber. Five years later the Peerage Act 1963 enabled the likes of Viscount Stansgate (Tony Benn MP) to renounce their hereditary title in order to be eligible to enter the House of Commons.

So what of the prospects of our entering the next century with an elected House of Lords? The last major attempt to reform the composition of the chamber occurred in 1969 with the introduction of the Parliament (No 2) Bill. This government proposal was defeated, however, by an 'unholy alliance' of right-wing Members of Parliament who wished to retain, if not enhance, the hereditary principle and left-wing Members of Parliament who feared that any constitutional reform of the House of Lords would ultimately lead to calls for the repeal of the Parliament Acts 1911 and 1949. The episode demonstrated that whatever the political will for change, there is little consensus on how best to reform the House of Lords. Moreover, due to its supportive role for the work of the House of Commons, there was little evidence of any political will to abolish the chamber in favour of unicameralism.

Elected chamber

There is little doubt, however, that the 'undemocratic' composition of the House of Lords is and will only continue to be tolerated because of the legislative supremacy of an elected House of Commons. But does the fact that the House of Commons is elected mean it is democratic, in the sense that its members may be said to truly represent the wishes of the electorate?

Consider the General Election Results from 1979 to 1997:

	1979	1983	1987	1992	1997
votes (%)	36.9	27.6	30.8	34.5	44.4
Labour seats (%)	42.2	32.2	35.2	41.6	63.6
votes (%)	43.9	42.4	42.2	41.9	31.4
Conservative seats (%)	53.4	61.1	57.8	51.6	25.0

votes (%)	13.8	25.4	22.6	17.9	17.2
Liberal Democrat (*)	1.7	3.5	3.4	3.1	7.0
seats (%)					
votes (%)	5.5	4.6	4.4	5.7	7.0
Others seats (%)	2.7	3.2	3.5	3.7	4.4

*   1979 – Liberal;

1983 and 1987 – Liberal/SDP;

1992 and 1997 – Liberal Democrats

It may be seen from these results that no government managed to achieve over 50% of the votes cast, yet always achieved over 50% of the seats in the House of Commons. The result for 1983 clearly demonstrates this point. By contrast, the Liberal Democrat (see above) vote always exceeded 10% but never secured 10% of the seats. Again the election result for 1983 demonstrates this point. The reason for these anomalies arises from the way in which our 'first-past-the-post' electoral system reflects strong centralised support within a constituency but fails to reflect support for parties diluted over a wide range of constituencies. The targeting of marginal constituencies in 1997 accounted for the Liberal Democrats doubling their number of seats from 1992 with a smaller percentage of the vote. Indeed, the Liberal Democrats now hold the most marginal constituency with a two vote margin of victory in Winchester.

Writing about the 1979 General Election in the *Sunday Times*, David Smith concluded that the three great elections of this century were the Liberal landslide in 1906; the post-war Labour landslide in 1945 and the 1997 Blair Labour landslide. The Conservative share of the vote (the lowest since 1832) still managed to secure more MPs than 1906 but for the first time failed to provide for a single MP in Scotland and in Wales (for the second time since 1906). Seven Cabinet Ministers lost their seats in the 1997 General Election beating 1945, when five, including the future Prime Minister, Harold MacMillan lost.

Deficiencies within the present system has led to calls from the minority parties for a more 'democratic' electoral system which more accurately reflects the voting pattern of the electorate. Systems of proportional representation have as their aim the correlation of figures for votes cast and seats won. This can be variously achieved, for example, through a party list system or the more widely preferred single transferable vote system. Whilst these systems would eradicate the anomalies inherent, for example, in the 1983 general election, they themselves are not without fault. In addition to being more complex, they require multi-member constituencies and traditionally result in coalition governments, where minority parties enjoy a political influence disproportionate to their votes.

Whatever the political promises for a Commission to investigate the merits of the case for reform of our electoral system, we must realistically accept that a party advantaged by the present system is unlikely to commit itself to changing it voluntarily. The question at issue, therefore, is whether the electorate feels itself sufficiently disadvantaged to make our electoral system in itself an electoral issue?

3 The citizen and the executive

You should be familiar with the following areas:

- Crown and Privy Council
- Royal Prerogative as a source of executive power
- Prime Minister and Cabinet
- Ministerial responsibility
- Civil Service

Introduction

Beating at the heart of any study of constitutional law are issues of power and accountability. It will be our task in this chapter to explore the reality of executive power and accountability. To this end we shall concentrate on the operation of central government.

You will note from Chapter 1 that we are said to have a constitution based upon the concept of parliamentary sovereignty. This means that we hold our legislature, as studied in Chapter 2, to be the supreme power within the State.

Yet, as we will see, for many commentators our constitution has evolved beyond this theoretical foundation to the extent that it is now not the legislature which controls the executive but rather the executive, through its domination of the party machine, which controls the legislature.

So what are the essential issues we will need address in this important exploration of power and accountability within our law of the constitution?

The Royal Prerogative

Sovereign power

At one time during our constitutional history the Monarch was the sovereign political power within the State through direct or indirect control of the executive, legislature and judiciary. The source of the Monarch's power was the Royal Prerogative, a term derived from the latin *pre* (before) and *rogo* (I demand). Thus the Royal Prerogative is what the Monarch demanded and was entitled to in preference to all others. The scope of the Monarch's absolute and discretionary powers became a matter for bitter dispute in Stuart times between royalist and parliamentary lawyers.

Prerogative power and the courts

In *Bate's Case* (1606) the Barons of the Exchequer found for King James I, when Bate refused to pay a tax on imported currants, on the basis that the regulation of foreign trade was ancillary to the King's prerogative in foreign affairs.

In the *Case of Prohibitions del Roy* (1607) it was noted by *Chief Justice Coke* that the King:

> In his own person cannot adjudge any case, either criminal ... or between party and party ... but this ought to be determined and adjudged in some court of justice.

The *Case of Proclamations* (1611) decided that the King:

> ... by his proclamation or other ways, cannot change any part of the common law or statute law, or the customs of the realm ... and the King cannot create any offence by his prohibition or proclamation which was not an offence before.

In *Darnel's Case* (1627) the response to a writ of *habeas corpus* that Darnel was imprisoned by special command of the King authorised by privy council warrant was deemed sufficient for the Judges.

In *R v Hampden* (1637) common law Judges found by majority for the King Charles I when Hampden refused to pay a tax. The tax, to create a navy to defend shipping had been authorised by the prerogative power for the defence of the realm but had not been sanctioned by Parliament. Hampden had argued that even if the King could raise taxes without reference to Parliament he could only do so where a real danger to the defence of the realm was proved.

The issue was still in dispute even after Civil War and the subsequent restoration of Monarchy. For example, in *Golden v Hales* (1686) Lord Chief Justice Herbert held that a dispensation granted by James II to a Colonel who became a Roman Catholic was a bar to any action under the Test Act.

Parliamentary sovereignty

The struggle between the Stuart monarchy and Parliament finally culminated in the removal of James II from the throne in the Glorious Revolution of 1688 and his replacement by William and Mary of Orange. The Bill of Rights 1689 placed the concept of the sovereignty of Parliament on a legal footing through the severe curtailment of the Royal Prerogative. It established as a general principle that prerogative powers can be either limited or abolished by statute.

The case of *AG v De Keyser's Royal Hotel* (1920) served to amplify this position. It was held in this case that Parliament may both expressly limit or abolish a prerogative and do so by implication. The latter is achieved by merely passing a statute which is inconsistent with the prerogative, although in such an instance the prerogative is only put into abeyance and presumably revives with the repeal of the statute. Moreover, in *R v Secretary of State for the Home Department, ex p Fire Brigades Union* (1995) the House of Lords affirmed the principle that the prerogative may not be employed to achieve an objective which is provided for under statutory powers. Thus, compensation payments under ss 108–17 of the Criminal Justice Act 1988 are now repealed by the Criminal Injuries Compensation Act 1995.

Crown

The aforementioned led Professor A V Dicey to conclude in his work, *Law of the Constitution* (1885) that:

> The prerogative appears to be both historically and as a matter of fact nothing less than the residue of discretionary and arbitrary authority, which at any given time is legally left in the hands of the Crown.

Many of these prerogative powers are today, however, not exercised by the Monarch in person but by other members of the executive in the name of the Crown. Even those prerogative powers which still remain within the personal domain of the Monarch, such as the dissolution of Parliament, the appointment of the Prime Minister, the dismissal of

Ministers and the granting of honours are constrained in their exercise by rules of convention.

Thus under the umbrella term of 'Crown', what was once the source of Royal power has in fact become an important tool of executive power. It was a recognition of this fact that lay behind the judgment of Lord Justice Diplock in *BBC v Johns* (1965) when he said:

> It is 350 years and a Civil War too late ... to broaden the prerogative. The limits within which the executive government may impose obligations or restraints on citizens of the United Kingdom without any statutory authority are now well settled and incapable of extension.

Sources of executive power

In the case *Council of Civil Service Unions v Minister for the Civil Service* (1985) the court followed the lead of Professor A V Dicey and used the term prerogative to cover all non-statutory actions of the executive.

By contrast, in his article entitled 'The "Third Source" of Authority for Government Action' (1992) *Law Quarterly Review*, B V Harris identifies three 'sources' of executive authority. The first source of authority is statute. The second is the prerogative as Professor Sir William Wade would understand it in 'the narrow sense', namely those ancient prerogatives which the courts through the common law have recognised as being unique to the Crown. The third is in actual fact not a source but rather a freedom, the freedom enjoyed by the Crown to do anything not prohibited by law. This freedom is the consequence of the principle of legality, that everything is legal which is not illegal.

Evidence of the third source can be seen in *Malone v Metropolitan Police Commissioner* (1979) where the authority for officers of the Crown to tap telephones stemmed from the fact that there is no right of privacy under our law and thus no law to prohibit the Crown tapping telephones (note the subsequent enactment of Interception of Communications Act 1985).

M v Home Office

To some Judges, such as Lord Diplock in *Town Investments v Dept of the Environment* (1978), executive use of the Royal Prerogative was such that the reality of the situation had now become that all actions of the executive were, 'acts done by "the Crown" in the fictional sense in which that expression is now used in English public law'.

This position, however, caused consternation in academic quarters. In his series of articles entitled, 'The Crown – Old Platitudes and New Heresies' (1992) *New Law Journal*, Professor Sir William Wade identified it as his first and perhaps most important heresy. He noted that in terms of executive action today the vast majority of powers, 'belong to Ministers, not to the Crown, and this fact, combined with the non-immunity of Crown servants, forms the bedrock on which the rule of law stands'. His conclusion was that if Judges allow the legal distinction between the Crown and the government, as servants of the Crown, to be removed then the rule of law was itself at stake. He looked to *M v Home Office, ex p Baker* (1993), 'the most important case in constitutional law for the last 200 years and more', to settle the issue.

Needless to say, you are required to know this case in detail. A good summary of the issues addressed and decided by the case is given by Professor Anthony Bradley, who appeared as Counsel, in the *Solicitors Journal* for October 1993. In particular he asks you to analyse the 'short but powerful speech' of Lord Templeman and that of Lord Woolf who addressed the three issues of: the individual liability of Crown officers at common law, the meaning of 'civil proceedings' under the Crown Proceedings Act 1947 and the granting of injunctive relief under Rules of the Supreme Court Order 53.

Lord Templeman

Taking note of the fact that, 'Parliament makes the law, the executive carry the law into effect and the judiciary enforce the law', Lord Templeman held that:

> The expression "the Crown" has two meanings, namely the Monarch and the executive. In the 17th century Parliament established its supremacy over the Crown as Monarch, over the executive and over the judiciary ... parliamentary supremacy over the judiciary is only exercisable by statute. The judiciary enforce the law against individuals, against institutions and against the executive. The Judges cannot enforce the law against the Crown as Monarch because the Crown as Monarch can do no wrong but Judges enforce the law against the Crown as executive and against individuals who from time to time represent the Crown ... the submission that there is no power to enforce the law by injunction or contempt proceedings against a Minister in his official capacity would, if upheld, establish the proposition that the executive obey the law as a matter of grace and not as a matter of necessity, a proposition which would reverse the result of the Civil War.

He was not prepared, therefore, to follow the finding of Simon Brown J at first instance that, 'when it comes to the enforcement of its decisions the relationship between the executive and the judiciary must, in the end, be one of trust'.

Lord Woolf

With regard to the individual liability of officers of the Crown at common law, Lord Woolf held that they were subject to law, 'both in their official capacity (note distinction with the finding of the Court of Appeal) and as individuals ... They are also liable to the law of contempt of court'. Noting that the aim of the Crown Proceedings Act 1947 was to make it easier and not more difficult for individuals to sue government, he held that contrary to *Merricks v Heathcoat-Amory* (1955) this position is not affected by s 21(2) of the Crown Proceedings Act 1947 which only excludes injunctions brought in civil proceedings under the 1947 Act and not at common law.

In terms of the second issue addressed, that of civil proceedings under the 1947 Act, Lord Woolf concluded that despite the lack of injunctive relief, departments would be expected to observe any declarations made by the court and thus, 'the only problem concerns interim relief'.

The third issue considered by Lord Woolf is perhaps the most crucial aspect of *M v Home Office, ex p Baker* (1993), namely the finding that s 31(2) of the Supreme Court Act 1981 allows for both permanent and interim injunctions to be issued against government departments, Ministers and other Crown representatives in judicial review proceedings. In his article '*M v Home Office*: Government and the Judges' (1993) *Public Law*, Mark Gould concludes that whilst the case is of undoubted importance to constitutional law its effects will be more readily felt in administrative law for it has, 'made a new range of remedies available against Ministers'.

Do we have a Prime Ministerial or Cabinet system of government?

Richard Crossman

In his introduction to the *English Constitution* by Walter Bagehot in 1963, Richard Crossman confidently asserted that, 'the post-war epoch has seen the final transformation of Cabinet Government into Prime Ministerial government'. But was his confidence justified?

Certainly Lord Hailsham believed it was when he delivered The Dimbleby Lecture in 1972. In his lecture entitled 'Elective Dictatorship', Lord Hailsham traced the movement of power within our constitution from medieval Monarchy to modern democracy and noted:

> Until comparatively recently, Parliament consisted of two effective chambers. Now for most practical purposes it consists of one. Until recently, the powers of government within Parliament were largely controlled either by the opposition or by its own back-benchers. It is now largely in the hands of the government machine, so that the government controls Parliament and not Parliament the government ... So the sovereignty of Parliament has increasingly become, in practice, the sovereignty of the Commons, and the sovereignty of the Commons has increasingly become the sovereignty of the government, which, in addition to its influence in Parliament, controls the party whips, the party machine, and the civil service.

This led Lord Hailsham to conclude that, 'we live under an elective dictatorship, absolute in theory, if hitherto thought tolerable in practice'. But what evidence is there to justify such a conclusion?

Cabinet government

Certainly few could doubt the growth of cabinet government. The origins of Cabinet government lie in the late 17th century and the creation, by Charles II, of a small *cabal* of Privy Counsellors in order to alleviate the frustration of working through the full Privy Council. Thus, far from being created by statute, the Cabinet, as an institution, merely evolved out of the Privy Council and is still technically one of its Committees.

At this time the members of the Cabinet were important court officials and not responsible to Parliament. However, in the 18th century parliamentary power steadily increased and it became politically expedient for the Monarch to choose as close advisers politicians with sufficient influence to secure the passage of measures, and especially financial measures, through the legislature.

By the time of the Reform Acts of 1832 and 1867 the power of the Monarch to appoint Ministers without taking the advice of leading parliamentary figures was effectively lost. With the expansion in the electorate came a growth in party politics. The Cabinet then began to emerge as the dominant political body within the constitution, representing in government the collective leadership of the party which was able to command a majority in the House of Commons.

From this growing dominance of the Cabinet emerged two new conventions of the constitution which are crucial to the working of modern Cabinet government. The first is that Ministers of the Crown are accountable, both collectively and individually, to Parliament. The second, that the Crown must only act as Ministers advise it to act.

Prime Minister

Out of the prominent party figures within the Cabinet, however, a leading figure would inevitably be recognised. It is from this that the office of the Prime Minister evolved. Thus, as with the Cabinet, the office of Prime Minister originated as a *de facto* (in fact) institution as opposed to one created *de jure* (in law). It exists by convention of the constitution and its powers are similarly only defined by convention.

Originally acknowledged as being merely *primus inter pares* (first amongst equals) and associated with the position of First Lord of the Treasury, the office has continued to grow in constitutional importance. In his book, *The Hidden Wiring: Unearthing the British Constitution* (1995), Professor Peter Hennessy set out to uncover the 'hidden wiring' that makes our constitutional machinery work. The three main strands he identifies are the Private Secretary to the Queen, the Principal Private Secretary to the Prime Minister and the Cabinet Secretary and concludes that virtually the whole weight of governing the country is now placed upon the shoulders of the Prime Minister. It is hardly surprising, therefore, that the office has attracted the criticism that it detracts from the power of the Cabinet. Even Prime Ministerial attempts at badly needed reforms of the Cabinet have attracted such criticism.

Reforms of Lloyd George

In 1916, for example, when Lloyd George became Prime Minister his major reforms of the central machinery of government attracted much adverse comment. With the country already committed to fighting the First World War he saw the need to create a small War Cabinet of five members serviced by a new Cabinet Office. The Cabinet Office contained within it a new secretariat which was responsible for producing agenda and minutes. Up until this time it was a convention that no minutes be kept of Cabinet deliberations for fear of inhibiting free and open discussion.

Reforms of Margaret Thatcher

In Margaret Thatcher's (now Lady Thatcher) administrations from 1979 to 1990 we again saw major reforms of the central machinery of government. This led to much speculation about the growth in Prime Ministerial power at the expense of the Cabinet. In particular the following reforms may be highlighted:

Civil service department

1968 was an important year for the reform of our civil service with the publication of the Fulton Report. This is a matter we will address later in this Chapter. However, it is important for us to note here that one of the reforms was the creation of a civil service department with responsibility for the operation of the civil service. One of Mrs Thatcher's early reforms in 1981 involved the abolition of this department and the allocation of some of its most important powers to the office of Prime Minister. Thus in addition to holding the title First Lord of the Treasury the Prime Minister also acquired the title Minister for the Civil Service (see GCHQ case).

Central Policy Review Staff (Think Tank)

Another reform in 1983 saw the abolition of the Central Policy Review Staff (CPRS), colloquially known as the 'Think Tank'. It is noted in, *Cabinet Government* by the Constitutional Reform Centre (1988) that the CPRS had been created by Sir Edward Heath's government in 1971 in order to help the Cabinet, to which it was directly responsible, '... rise above narrow department perspectives ... (and) ... think strategically rather than tactically'. However, it depended for its very existence on the goodwill of the Prime Minister and by 1983 its attempts, 'to adapt to a new Prime Ministerial style had clearly failed'.

Prime Minister's Office

The most significant reform was the reorganisation of 10 Downing Street. There has always been a constitutional distinction between the Cabinet Office, as created by Lloyd George and any personal staff of the Prime Minister. Yet in order to avoid charges of Prime Ministerial dictatorship it had become common practice for Premiers to place some of their senior advisers in the Cabinet Office. Mrs Thatcher, however, formed her own Prime Minister's Office which incorporated a Political Office, Private Office, Policy Unit, Efficiency Unit and a Press Office.

The origins of the Political Office lay in Harold Wilson's (now Lord Wilson) appointment of Marcia Williams (now Lady Falkender) as his 'personal and political secretary' in 1964. Staffed by non-civil servants its function was to keep the Prime Minister in contact with current thinking within the parliamentary party.

The Private Office had at its head a Principal Private Secretary with other senior staff normally on secondment from departments in Whitehall. In addition to operating the engagements diary, the office was responsible for briefing the Prime Minister and most of the official paperwork of 10 Downing Street.

The most controversial development, however, was the growth in influence of the Policy Unit. Established by Harold Wilson in 1974, the Unit was responsible for directly advising the Prime Minister on a whole range of policy areas. Despite the fact that it was made up of a mix of outside appointments and civil servants, the advice it tendered was independent of and often contrary to that given to Ministers by their respective departments.

It is this fact that ultimately led to the resignation of the Chancellor of the Exchequer, Nigel Lawson (now Lord Lawson) in October 1989. Nigel Lawson felt his position became untenable when Mrs Thatcher refused to accede to his request to dismiss Sir Alan Walters, her adviser on economic and financial matters, for publicly tendering advice which was contrary to his own.

The Efficiency Unit was introduced to initiate reforms of the civil service for the benefit of efficiency gain. Originally headed by Lord Rayner from Marks & Spencer plc, the intention was to apply business practices to running the central administration.

Lastly, there was the Press Office headed by a Chief Press Secretary. Usually this was a fairly anonymous figure but Mrs Thatcher's Chief Press Secretary, the now Sir Bernard Ingham, became a somewhat controversial figure through his strong support of her views and criticism of some Ministers. In particular, members of the Cabinet not in support of the Prime Minister's monetarist policies were portrayed to the media as 'wets'.

Final transition?

The aforementioned led some commentators to conclude that the Thatcher premiership was the final transition into Prime Ministerial government. Writing in the *Guardian* newspaper in November 1988 Richard Holmes, Editor of the Constitutional Reform Centre, warned that we now had a constitution in shambles:

> As government presses on towards the very limits of partisanship, the frail conventions which once provided at least the illusion of consent to cover the naked exercise of power, have one by one been ripped away.

Yet if Mrs Thatcher's administrations provide evidence to support the assertions of Richard Crossman and Lord Hailsham that we now have Prime Ministerial government, so to does her fall from grace demonstrate the significance of the Cabinet.

Leadership contest

In 1990 Michael Heseltine, who had previously resigned from the Cabinet in 1986 during what became known as the 'Westland Affair', stood against Mrs Thatcher for the leadership of the Conservative party. The rules for such a contest dated from 1965 and the controversial appointment by the Monarch of Sir Alec Douglas-Home to succeed the then Harold Macmillan as Prime Minister. They allowed for Conservative Members of Parliament to hold an annual election, organised by the backbench 1922 Committee, even when the present leader was the sitting Prime Minister.

The rules allowed for up to three ballots. If the existing leader failed to secure an overall majority of those eligible to vote plus a clear 15% more (of those eligible to vote) than any other candidate, then a second ballot was to be held. In the next ballot there was only a requirement to secure a majority of those eligible to vote. Failure to achieve this resulted in a third and final ballot, where only the top three candidates from the second ballot would be allowed to stand. Each Member of Parliament would then have two votes based on first and second preference to ensure the overall majority.

In November 1990 there were 372 Members of Parliament in receipt of the Conservative whip, therefore to win an overall majority required 187 votes and 15% more than any other candidate amounted to 56 more votes. The result of the first ballot was as follows:

Margaret Thatcher	204 votes
Michael Heseltine	152 votes
Abstentions	16

Thus Mrs Thatcher had secured the first requirement of gaining an overall majority but had failed, by four votes, to secure the second requirement. It is at this stage that the influence of the Cabinet may be seen. It was made clear to the Prime Minister through meeting each member of the Cabinet individually that she no longer enjoyed its support. It was then that she decided to withdraw from the second ballot, which allowed John Major to secure the leadership of the Conservative party as follows:

John Major   185 votes
Michael Heseltine 131 votes
Douglas Hurd   56 votes

(*Note* Mrs Thatcher still remained as Prime Minister until John Major
    was appointed as such by the Queen.)

Crossman refuted?

In his book entitled *Thatcherism and British Politics: the End of Consensus*
(1990) Professor Kavanagh concluded that, 'it is very difficult to imag-
ine a Prime Minister in good health being deposed by Cabinet colleagues'. Yet for many the role of the Cabinet in Lady Thatcher's
removal from power had been crucial and demanded a reassessment
of the importance of the Cabinet.

In his article, 'The End of Prime Ministerial Government?' (1991)
Public Law, Professor Geoffrey Marshall went further by stating:

> Given that British Prime Ministers, unlike American Presidents,
> are so obviously dependent upon the continued support of their
> party majorities and Cabinet colleagues, one might wonder how it
> could ever have come to be plausibly asserted that, 'the post-war
> epoch has seen the final transformation of Cabinet government
> into Prime Ministerial government'.

Professor Marshall warns that, 'perhaps some caution is necessary in
assessing the views of Cabinet Ministers, especially those who are dis-
gruntled or disappointed in office, since they may be tempted to see (a
Prime Ministerial) dictatorship where their own views are overruled'.

Harold Wilson, who was the Prime Minister at the time that Richard
Crossman was a Minister, like Lord Gordon-Walker, believed that 'the
Cabinet in Parliament' was still the central feature of executive power.
This is not to say, however, that the Prime Minister is without major
constitutional power or significance today.

Ministerial responsibility

So far we have explored the sources and exercise of executive power.
Now we need to consider the accountability of the executive under our
constitution. This is again determined by a convention, that of ministerial responsibility. This convention has two parts, collective responsibility and individual responsibility.

Collective responsibility

It is one of the central features of our evolutionary constitution that Parliament, through the concept of its own supremacy and corresponding reduction in the powers of the Monarch, has been able to assert the accountability of the government as a whole to Parliament. This collective responsibility owed to Parliament takes two forms.

Government must resign if it loses the support of the elected chamber

An example of this would be the resignation of the James Callaghan (now Lord Callaghan) government in 1979 and the consequent General Election. Understanding this part of the convention is crucial to an appreciation of its significance to the operation of our constitution. It goes to the very heart of the relationship between our legislature and executive. For example, on 13 October 1992 Michael Heseltine, as President of the Board of Trade announced the government's intention to close 31 coal pits. Given that this announcement was made with the support of the Prime Minister and Cabinet one might have thought that the issue was settled. Yet he was forced to abandon, if only temporarily, this policy initiative after it became apparent that there was strong hostility to the measure in Parliament. Yet this is not to say that the convention is a major constitutional constraint on executive power. It actually serves to strengthen the position of the executive. Thus when John Major and his Cabinet suffered a defeat by 324 votes to 316 in Parliament on 22 July 1992 (largely at the hands of 23 backbench rebels) on a motion relating to the Maastricht Treaty on European Union, he was able to restore his authority by putting down a motion of confidence for the following day. The motion inevitably secured a majority as the rebels within his party knew that its defeat would have led to the dissolution of Parliament and the possibility of the Labour party winning the subsequent General Election.

Government must speak with one voice

The second form which collective responsibility takes can also serve to enhance the position of the Prime Minister. If government is to be made accountable to Parliament then the action for which it is held to be responsible must be clear. Such clarity can only be achieved by the government speaking with but one voice. This part of the convention has a crucial bearing on the operation of the Cabinet.

By convention civil service advice to Cabinet Ministers is confidential, as is the ensuing discussion between Ministers themselves. But whatever the advice or discussion, once the government's position has been made clear, all members of the Cabinet are held collectively responsible for it.

Thus a Minister in the minority opinion in Cabinet has but three options: either to accept and publicly defend the decision, tender his resignation or seek to breach the convention by secretly briefing the media on his disquiet with government policy.

The latter course is not, however, without political danger. Prime Ministers jealously guard this part of the convention as a mechanism by which they can 'muzzle' opponents from within the Cabinet. However, the political reality of a given situation can cause even a Prime Minister to give ground. For example, to avoid the possibility of mass resignation and the political embarrassment it would cause, Harold Wilson once waived the operation of this part of the convention. It should be noted, however, that this 'agreement to differ' amongst Cabinet colleagues related only to the issue of continuing membership of the Common Market and the convention was fully restored after the referendum in 1975.

Individual responsibility

One of the important features of our civil service is its claim to political neutrality. Civil servants are meant to remain as the anonymous advisers of government Ministers. It is felt that without such anonymity their position of permanency within our constitution would be threatened.

Thus a Minister is expected to accept a responsibility for the protection of his civil servant advisers. This means that a Minister is not only responsible to Parliament in a collective sense for the policies of the government as a whole but is also responsible, in an individual sense, for his own actions and those of his department. But are Ministers constitutionally accountable to Parliament for every action undertaken by his civil servants?

When are Ministers under a duty to accept responsibility for the actions of their civil servants?

This question was central to what has become known as the, 'Crichel Down Affair'. In 1939 the Air Ministry compulsorily acquired Crichel Down, an area of farmland in Dorset. After the Second World War the land was transferred to the Ministry of Agriculture who refused a request from the previous owners to re-purchase it. This refusal was accompanied by misleading replies and the matter was taken up in Parliament. Following an Inquiry which found 'inefficiency, bias and bad faith' on the part of some officials, five of whom were named, the Minister, Sir Thomas Dugdale, resigned.

The most important constitutional aspect of this affair is the subsequent statement by the Home Secretary, Sir David Maxwell-Fyfe in the House of Commons, on when a Minister must accept responsibility for the actions of his civil servants. The Home Secretary made clear that such a constitutional duty existed where the civil servant was carrying out either government policy or the explicit orders of the Minister. If a civil servant caused delay or made a mistake, but not on a major issue of policy or where individual rights are seriously affected, the Minister must again acknowledge responsibility and ensure that corrective action is taken within the department. The Minister was deemed not to be under such a constitutional duty where, otherwise than above, the Minister had no previous knowledge and disapproved of the action taken by the civil servant. This leads us to the issue of, having accepted responsibility for the actions of his civil servants: when is a Minister is under an obligation to resign?

When is a Minister under a duty to resign?

It is, perhaps, much to the credit of our civil service that the vast majority of ministerial resignations in the last few years have resulted from the actions of Ministers and Cabinet colleagues rather than their civil servants.

For example, between 1982 and 1994 there were four ministerial resignations resulting from injudicious comments or claims by Ministers taken up by the media: 1982 Nicholas Fairburn (failure to prosecute in a rape case), 1988 Edwina Currie (salmonella in eggs), 1990 Nicholas Ridley (adverse comments about Germans and the European Community), 1993 Michael Mates (inscription on a watch to Asil Nadir, a fraud suspect). A similar number involved Ministers having extra-marital affairs: 1983 Cecil Parkinson, 1992 David Mellor, 1994 Tim Yeo and Lord Caithness.

Yet in the same period there were only two instances where Ministers have, in part at least, accepted responsibility for the actions of their civil servants and resigned. In the first instance Lord Carrington and his team of Ministers at the Foreign Office resigned in 1982 after the invasion by Argentina of the Falkland Islands. In the second, and as part of the 'Westland Affair', Sir Leon Brittan resigned in 1986 after it was revealed that his department had disclosed to the media parts of a letter from the Solicitor General to Michael Heseltine, with the intention of discrediting the latter.

Interestingly, there were more instances, in the same period, of Ministers not resigning. Whereas Lord Carrington left the Foreign Office, John Nott (now Sir John Nott) was persuaded by the Prime Minister not to resign from the Ministry of Defence. James Prior (now Lord Prior) was similarly persuaded in 1983 not to resign as Secretary of State for Northern Ireland, after the escape of 38 republican prisoners from the Maze prison. In the following year Kenneth Baker refused to resign his position as Home Secretary after the escape of two IRA remand prisoners from Brixton Prison. Kenneth Baker again refused to resign when he was held in contempt of court in *M v Home Office, ex p Baker* (1993). In his view no duty was owed as he was only following the particular course of action because of the legal advice he had received from departmental lawyers and Treasury Counsel.

In her article, 'Ministerial Responsibility: The Abdication of Responsibility Through the Receipt of Legal Advice' (1993) *Public Law*, which followed an earlier article, 'Ministerial Responsibility in the 1990s: When Do Ministers Resign?' published in *Parliamentary Affairs*, Diana Woodhouse argued that this, and other instances, demonstrate a growing and constitutionally dangerous trend. In 1992 four Ministers involved in the 'Matrix Churchill Affair', Michael Heseltine, Kenneth Clarke, Malcolm Rifkind and Tristan Garel-Jones, again justified their actions on the basis of legal advice for which they did not hold themselves responsible. The Attorney-General, Sir Nicholas Lyell, took the unusual step of informing the media that his advice to the Ministers was that, 'they were required by law to claim public interest immunity' and that such a claim 'could not be waived'.

Diana Woodhouse notes that it has been accepted since the time of Balfour in 1901 that, '... law officers have no control over the legal actions of the government'. Whether Ministers follow legal advice is a matter for them. Kenneth Baker, for example:

> ... knew, or should have known, that to ignore the (court) order, even if legally justified, would be controversial, both because it flouted the authority of the court and because of the possible consequences for the individual concerned. The more appropriate action would have been to ensure the return of the deportee and then challenge the validity of the order.

So are Ministers being allowed to get away with not resigning from office when there is a constitutional duty to do so? In an article for *Public Administration* in 1956 entitled, 'The Individual Responsibility of Ministers', Professor S E Finer concluded that resignations will only occur if, 'the Minister is yielding, his Prime Minister unbending, and his party is out for blood'.

Certainly these are three factors that need to be taken into account. If Ministers, for whatever reason, are intent on resigning then they will go, eg Sir Thomas Dugdale, Lord Carrington, Sir Geoffrey Howe (now Lord Howe), Michael Heseltine, Nigel Lawson (now Lord Lawson). But many of the resignations to which we have referred involved Ministers who clearly did not intend to yield. David Mellor, for example, went on *News At Ten* to say that he would not be resigning and that it was the Prime Minister who chose the Cabinet not the media, just hours before his departure from the Heritage department.

Once a Minister loses the support of the Prime Minister then defeat is inevitable. At the time of Britain's expensive and undignified withdrawal from the ERM in September 1992 John Major protected Norman Lamont by taking, 'full responsibility for the actions and policies of the Chancellor'. Within a few months, however, the Prime Minister considered Mr Lamont's position at the Treasury to be no longer tenable and he was manoeuvred into resigning. This is not to say, however, that the support of the Prime Minister guarantees the Minister's survival. John Major continued to give strong support to David Mellor, a personal friend, but as we have seen was not able to sustain him in office.

Diana Woodhouse confirms, 'that resignations are less a product of constitutional morality than of party management'. As with any conventional rule of our constitution the issue becomes one of enforcement. If Ministers are in a constitutional sense 'getting away' with not resigning, then ultimately the problem lies with the party in power at Westminster.

The Civil Service

Issues of accountability have also come to the fore in the recent academic debate on dramatic organisational changes to the structure and running of our civil service. In the parliamentary session 1987–88 the Treasury and Civil Service Select Committee reported that changes proposed to the civil service by the Efficiency Unit, 'could be the most far-reaching since the Northcote-Trevelyan Reforms in the 19th century'.

First Steps Initiative

Originally led by Lord Rayner, the Efficiency Unit, by the time of Mrs Thatcher's third successive election victory in 1987, was now under the control of Sir Robin Ibbs. The Ibbs proposal was that the devolved budgeting principles inherent in the Financial Management Initiative introduced by his predecessor in 1982 should be followed up in 1988 with the launch of, 'Improving Management in Government: The Next Steps Initiative'.

The basis of the proposal was that 95% of civil service activity was concerned with public service delivery, which could be provided more effectively by 'hiving off' such administrative functions to new executive agencies. The Fulton Report of 1968 had also given a cautious welcome to the possibility of 'hiving-off' but by 1977 the old Expenditure Committee was warning that it was, 'only viable in limited areas of government ... and should be approached with caution ... hiving off necessarily involves a diminution in the area of Ministerial control'.

Ten years on and such concerns were put to one side when the Prime Minister, Margaret Thatcher, announced the appointment of Peter Kemp to the Office of the Minister for the Civil Service as Project Officer overseeing the implementation of the Next Steps Initiative. The committed aim was to:

> Establish a quite different way of conducting the business of government. The central Civil Service should consist of a relatively small core engaged in the function of servicing Ministers and managing departments, who will be the 'sponsors' of particular government policies and services. Responding to these departments will be a range of agencies employing their own staff ... and concentrating on the delivery of their particular service.

When pressed on the point by Terence Higgins, Chairman of the Treasury and Civil Service Committee, the Prime Minister sought to reassure that there would be, 'no change in the arrangements for accountability'. Yet in a series of articles on this issue Professor Gavin Drewry poses the fundamental question:

> How can Ministers credibly cling to their virtual monopoly of accountability to Parliament, via traditional models of ministerial responsibility that (according to the Prime Minister) are to remain unaltered by 'The Next Steps', in respect of semi-autonomous agencies whose chief executives are expected to take managerial initiatives at arm's length from ministerial control?

The significance of the question became all the more apparent in 1995 when, after sacking Derek Lewis (its Director-General) the Home Secretary refused to accept individual responsibility for the running of the prison service. Michael Howard sought to separate 'policy' considerations from 'operational' matters, which were the sole responsibility of the Prisons Board. 1995 also saw the publication of the Next Steps Review. Sir Peter Kemp would note that with over 100 agencies now in existence the review shows that, 'this eight year old child is healthy ... (although) ... there is some way to go yet'.

Sir Robin Butler, the Cabinet Secretary, gave the first clue that Ministers were backing away from their traditional obligations when he informed the Scott Inquiry that there was a difference between ministerial responsibility to Parliament and ministerial 'accountability'. Indeed, Sir Robert went further and suggested 'accountability' could be a blame-free word. The Treasury and Civil Service Select Committee, in its fifth Report on the role of the Civil Service, felt this to be a novel constitutional doctrine which it found 'unconvincing'. According to Elizabeth Symons, General Secretary of the Association of First Division Civil Servants, 'the problem is that Ministers are quick to take the credit and slow to take any blame and we really need to sort out the question of responsibility and accountability'. The solution proposed by the General Secretary is to have a Civil Service Act, so that civil servants might know exactly what is to be expected of them.

4 The citizen and judicial control of the abuse of power

You should be familiar with the following areas:

- nature and scope of administrative law
- procedure for making an application for a judicial review
- grounds for making an application for a judicial review
- public and private law remedies
- public interest immunity claims and ouster clauses

Introduction

No study of constitutional law would be complete without a study of administrative law, yet the definition and scope of both, together with public law in general, is open to interpretation.

In Chapter 1 we recognise that we have an evolving constitution, theoretically based on the concept of parliamentary sovereignty. In Chapter 2 we note that Parliament is bicameral and that it is the elected chamber, the House of Commons, which dominates the House of Lords. In Chapter 3 we acknowledge that constitutional law addresses issues of power and accountability within a State. We then traced the transference of power within our State from Monarchy and the legislature to the executive. In this Chapter we focus on the mechanism of judicial review, which allows for Judges to make our executive legally accountable for its actions.

Administrative law may be said to have grown from the development of the administrative State. At one time the prevailing philosophy was *laissez-faire* (let it be). To the economist this means a free market economy but for the lawyer it means non-intervention by the State. Society then moved to the philosophy of a Welfare State, where the

State actively intervenes to provide basic welfare services for its citizens. Such welfare services need to be administered by the State and its agencies. Out of this grew administrative law, in order to regulate disputes between citizens and their State arising from the administration of these services.

Whether the growth in administrative law arose from a fear of State interventionism or the need to facilitate better administrative decisions on the part of the State is open to question. What we can say is that this growth is comparatively recent and seemingly unprecedented in scale. In his article, 'Judicial Review: A Possible Programme for Reform' (1992) *Public Law*, Lord Woolf reaffirmed that:

> I find it difficult to believe that there has been any other period in our legal history where a sphere of law has developed in such a rapid and exciting manner as administrative law over the period since I started practice.

So what are the essential issues we need to address in our study of this dynamic area of the course?

What is judicial review?

Public law

The distinction between public law and private law is fundamental to many legal systems and in particular those whose origins lie in Roman law. Public law is that body of law which directly relates to the State and its relationship with its citizens. The body of private law within a State regulates the relationships between its citizens.

Administrative law

Professor Sir William Wade asserts in *Administrative Law* (1988) that administrative law can be said to contain the body of general principles which govern the exercise of powers and duties by public bodies. Further, that it is the law relating to the control of governmental power which has as its primary purpose:

> ... to keep the powers of government within their legal bounds, so as to protect the citizen against their abuse. The powerful engines of authority must be prevented from running amok.

Constitutional law

Administrative law therefore addresses public law issues. But so to does constitutional law, so what, if any, difference is there between them? For *Professor Sir William Wade*:

> The whole of administrative law ... may be treated as a branch of constitutional law, since it flows directly from the constitutional principles of the rule of law, the sovereignty of parliament and the independence of the judiciary; and it does much to determine the balance of power between the State and the citizen.

Judicial review

A detailed study of administrative law would require a consideration of administrative rules and procedures, the work of administrative tribunals, inquiries and ombudsfolk system. But at the core of any study of administrative law lies judicial review and it is to this area that we must now turn our attention.

Judicial review relates to the granting of the prerogative orders of *certiorari, mandamus* and prohibition. These prerogative powers were historically used by the Council of the King to supervise the work of justices of the peace who had both judicial and administrative responsibilities within localities.

With the growth of the administrative State these supervisory powers, which were now in the hands of Judges of the Queen's Bench Division, started to acquire ever-increasing importance. By 1929 Lord Chief Justice Hewart was beginning to express judicial concern at 'The New Despotism'. In particular, there was increasing unease with the growth of delegated legislation and the wide discretionary powers Parliament was granting to Ministers. Such concern ultimately led to an investigation by the Donoughmore-Scott Committee into Ministers' powers. A good illustration of the powers now being conferred on Ministers by Parliament is found in the Deregulation and Contracting Out Act 1994. The vast powers given to Ministers for the granting of deregulation orders under Part I of the Act were described by the Delegated Powers Scrutiny Committee as being 'unprecedented in times of peace'. Thus, whereas citizens are asked to accept delegated legislation as a necessary evil, it is recognised that the judiciary have an important role to play in ensuring that an ever powerful executive acts within its legal constraints.

What bodies are subject to judicial review?

The fundamental question of what bodies are subject to judicial review is in such a state of present confusion and uncertainty as to render it a prime area for a question in the examination. Judicial use of the prerogative orders of *mandamus, certiorari* and prohibition is discretionary and it is the Judges themselves who have set the limitations and direction of judicial review.

In 1923 Lord Justice Atkin held in *R v Electricity Commissioners, ex p London Electricity Joint Committee* (1924) that: 'any body of persons having legal authority to determine questions affecting the rights of subjects, and having the duty to act judicially' were susceptible to an application for a judicial review. The continuing growth of the administrative State and a judicial desire for greater use of judicial review called into question the limitations imposed by Lord Atkin.

By 1964 the legal distinction between having a duty to act judicially, as opposed to a mere administrative duty, was effectively removed by Lord Reid in *Ridge v Baldwin* (1964).

The next development occurred three years later in 1967. Up until that time judicial review was confined to those inferior bodies to which Parliament had delegated powers (*vires*). It was the task of the court, through judicial review, to ensure that these inferior bodies remained within their powers (*intra vires*) and did not go beyond either the express or implied limits of their power (*ultra vires*). The implied limits on their power were set by Judges and known as the 'Wednesbury principles' (*Associated Provincial Picture Houses v Wednesbury Corpn* (1948)).

In *R v Criminal Injuries Board, ex p Lain* (1967), however, judicial review was extended to include bodies acting pursuant to prerogative powers. This development was affirmed by Judges of the House of Lords in *Council of Civil Service Unions v Minister for the Civil Service* (1985). Although the court went on to identify areas relating to the prerogative where judicial review would not be used ('the making of Treaties, the defence of the realm, the prerogative of mercy, the grant of honours, the dissolution of Parliament and the appointment of Ministers ...') it was subsequently decided by Lord Justice Watkins in *R v Home Secretary, ex p Bentley* (1993) that the prerogative of mercy was subject to judicial review and, 'it will be for other courts to decide on a case by case basis whether (other aspects are) reviewable or not ...'.

Thus Judges no longer confine the jurisdiction of judicial review to inferior bodies acting outside their *vires*. Instead, we are told by Lord

Templeman in *R v ITC, ex p TSW Broadcasting* (1992) that Judges 'invented the remedy of judicial review ... to ensure that the decision-maker did not (either) exceed or abuse his powers'. But the question still remains, which decision-makers are susceptible to an application for a judicial review?

In 1986 Judges in the Court of Appeal held the decisions of a city Panel on Take-overs and Mergers to be subject to judicial review. *R v Panel on Take-Overs and Mergers, ex p Datafin* (1987) represents a major development for it was recognised by the Judges that the Panel had 'no statutory, prerogative or common law powers' and so performed its functions, 'without visible means of legal support'.

We may therefore say that public body decision-makers acting under statutory powers are subject to judicial review, as are public body decision-makers acting under prerogative powers, subject to certain limitations. But according to *R v Panel on Take-overs and Mergers, ex p Datafin* (1987) so to is any private body decision-maker, subject to the nature of their decision.

This blurring of the significance of the type of body taking the decision may be controversial but is growing in importance when one considers the recent government policy of taking bodies out of the public sector for the intended purpose of efficiency gain.

We have already noted that since the 1980s we have seen a revolution in the administration of many sectors of government activity. The civil service has undergone a programme of radical reform with the Next Steps Initiative and the growth of 'executive agencies' (eg Driver Vehicle Licensing Agency, United Kingdom Passport Agency). The National Health Service is undergoing major managerial reform with the National Health Service and Community Care Act 1990 and 'Trust Status Hospitals'. The function of Local Authorities has been transformed. Local Education Authority Colleges in the Further and Higher Education sector have been given 'Corporate Status'. Most publicly owned Corporations have been 'privatised' (eg British Telecom and all the utilities such as electricity, gas and water).

Many of these privatised industries have had 'regulatory agencies' imposed upon them such as OFTEL (telephones), OFFER (electricity), OFGAS (gas), OFWAT (water). These new bodies join other regulatory agencies prescribed by statute or prerogative such as the Civil Aviation Authority, Commission For Racial Equality, Equal Opportunities Commission, Independent Television Commission, Monopolies And Mergers Commission, the Welsh Development Agency etc all variously described as quangos (quasi-autonomous non-governmental bodies), fringe bodies or non-departmental public bodies. In addition to these prescribed regulatory bodies there are voluntary or self-regulatory agencies such as the Panel on Take-overs and Mergers, the Advertising Standards Authority and various sporting bodies such as the Jockey Club and Football Association.

Whereas it is clear that government policy is to move bodies from the public sector, what is perhaps not so clear is where these bodies are being moved to. However, for the purposes of judicial review *R v Panel on Take-overs and Mergers, ex p Datafin* (1987) requires that emphasis is placed on the nature of the decision itself rather than the type of body making the decision.

What decisions are subject to judicial review?

The judgment of *Sir John Donaldson*, Master of the Rolls, in *R v Panel on Take-Overs and Mergers, ex p Datafin* (1987) makes clear that, 'the only essential elements are what can be described as a public element ... and the exclusion (of) ... a consensual submission to ... jurisdiction'.

'Public element'?

It is clear from *R v East Berkshire Health Authority, ex p Walsh* (1985) and *R v Chief Rabbi, ex p Wachmann* (1992) that the requirement of the decision having a public element is not satisfied simply because the public is interested in the result. Justice Simon Brown said in the latter case, 'whether a decision has public law consequences must be determined otherwise than by reference to the seriousness of its impact upon those affected'.

It would also be wrong to assume that just because the decision-maker is a public body, namely a body created by Royal Prerogative, statute or statutory instrument that all its decisions are subject to judicial review. In *R v BBC, ex p Lavelle* (1983) and *R v East Berkshire Health Authority, ex p Walsh* (1985) the decisions of these public bodies were not susceptible to a judicial review because they related to employment matters within the private law domain. Likewise R *v IBA, ex p Rank* (1986) and *R v NCB, ex p NUM* (1986) where commercial decisions were not held to be reviewable.

Public bodies

In *R v Panel on Take-overs and Mergers, ex p Datafin* (1985), Lord Justice Lloyd states that, '... the source of the power will often, perhaps usually, be decisive'. The decisions of public bodies acting under statutory or prerogative authority are likely, therefore, to be presumed by Judges to have a public element unless it can be proved to the contrary. But what of non-public bodies?

Non-public bodies

Here Judges have adopted a simple 'but for' test. But for the existence of that non-public body, would the State be likely to have to enact legislation to confer statutory powers on a comparable body to regulate the area of life over which the non-public body has *de facto* control?

In *R v Chief Rabbi, ex p Wachmann* (1992) Justice Simon Brown concluded that the decisions of the Chief Rabbi were not subject to judicial review because:

> His functions are essentially intimate, spiritual and religious, functions which the government could not and would not seek to discharge in his place were he to abdicate his regulatory responsibility.

Exclusion of a consensual submission to jurisdiction?

It is a well-established principle that judicial review cannot be used to regulate the decisions of bodies with which the applicant has voluntarily entered into a consensual (contractual) relationship.

In his article, 'Who is Subject to Judicial Review and in Respect of What? (1992) *Public Law*, David Pannick argues that this principle has been misapplied by Judges in some of the applications involving sporting bodies. In particular, he cites the decision of Lord Justice Neill in *R v Disciplinary Committee of the Jockey Club, ex p Massingberd-Mundy* (1990) where decisions of the Jockey Club were held not to be susceptible to judicial review because, 'owners, trainers and riders of horses as well as executives of the various race courses have a contractual relationship with the Jockey Club and have agreed to be bound by the rules of racing'. This precedent was then reluctantly followed in *R v Jockey Club, ex p RAM Racecourses* (1990) leaving the then Lord Justice Woolf feeling obliged to follow the preceding cases in *R v Disciplinary Committee of the Jockey Club, ex p Aga Khan* (1993), despite accepting that the decisions of the Jockey Club were of, 'public interest and public importance'.

In his article, 'Pitch, Pool, Rink ... Court? Judicial Review in the Sporting World' (1989) *Public Law*, Michael Beloff believes it is, 'the floodgates argument that is the unspoken premise' of precedents relating to sporting bodies '... the fear that limited court time will be absorbed by a new and elastic category of case with much scope for abusive or captious litigation'. For Michael Beloff, 'it is an argument which intellectually has little to commend it and pragmatically is usually shown to be ill-founded'.

It is suggested by David Pannick that the better course is to follow the views expressed by Justice Simon Brown in *R v Chief Rabbi, ex p Wachmann* (1992) where he rejected the argument that the Chief Rabbi is not subject to judicial review because, 'no one is compelled to be a Jew, or Orthodox Jew, still less a Rabbi', for as he explained, 'an Orthodox Rabbi is pursuing a vocation and has no choice but to accept the Chief Rabbi's disciplinary decisions'.

In the recent decision of *R v Lloyds of London, ex p Briggs* (1993) Lord Justice Leggatt and Justice Popplewell may be seen to offer support for this proposition. They held that one of the reasons why Lloyds of London was not amenable to a judicial review was because it did not enjoy a monopolistic position within the insurance market. Its powers were derived from statute, the Lloyds Act 1871, but this was a Private Act which did not:

> ... extend to any persons other than those who wish to operate within one section of the market and who have committed themselves by entering into the uniform contract prescribed by the respondent (Lloyd's).

One might argue, therefore, that judicial review should not be excluded for reasons of 'consensual submission' where the relevant body has monopolistic powers which the applicant has to accept if he wishes to participate in the area of life governed by the body in question.

The procedure for making an application for a judicial review

Order 53

The initial concern of any litigant in administrative law is which procedure should be adopted to commence an action. In essence the two types of procedure available reflect the public law and private law divide. An application for a judicial review will have the High Court as the court of first instance. Thus the procedure to be adopted is prescribed in the *Rules of the Supreme Court* (White Book). In particular, Order 53 (Ord 53) contains the rules relating to an application for a judicial review.

Up until 1977 this procedure did not allow for cross-examination on affidavits, discovery, interrogatories or the private law remedies of damages, declaration or injunction to be added to the claim for the pre-rogative orders of *mandamus*, *certiorari* and prohibition. Responding to the Law Commission Report 'Remedies in Administrative Law 1976' these deficiencies were removed by Rules of the Supreme Court (Amendment No 3) 1977 (SI 1977 No 1955).

In particular, Ord 53 r 7 allows a claim for damages if damages would have been available in an action started by writ, and Ord 53 r 8 allows for the discovery of documents, administering of interrogatories and cross-examination of deponents on affidavits. These procedural reforms were later enshrined in s 31 of the Supreme Court Act 1981.

The other procedural obstacles remained. The justification being that the courts needed greater control over public law proceedings than private law proceedings, that the essence of the public law proceeding was speed and that it was important to channel these actions to the specialist Judges assigned to the Crown Office list.

Leave and *locus standi*

Order 53 r 3 requires the obtaining of leave of the court. Order 53 r 3(7) only allows leave to be granted where the applicant has a sufficient interest, known by the latin tag *locus standi*. The leading decision of *R v IRC, ex p National Federation of Self-Employed and Small Businesses* (1982) establishes that the issue of sufficient interest may be considered at both the leave stage and at the hearing, although the test applied at the different stages may not be the same.

Undue delay

Order 53 r 4 requires that an application:

> ... shall be made promptly and in any event within three months from the date when grounds for the application first arose unless the court considers that there is good reason for extending the period.

In considering such an extension, Judges in the House of Lords made clear in *R v Diary Produce Quota Tribunal, ex p Caswell* (1990), that a court should have consideration of s 31(6) and (7) of the Supreme Court Act 1981. Thus no extension must be granted if the effect of granting the relief sought, 'would be likely to cause substantial hardship to, or substantially prejudice the rights of, any person or would be detrimental to good administration'.

This is not to say, however, that Ord 53 r 4 offers a three month limitation period. It was made equally clear by Judges in the High Court in *R v Swale BC, ex p RSPB* (1990) that an application for a judicial review can be struck out on the grounds of undue delay even when it is initiated within a three-month period.

Private law action

By contrast, private law actions against public bodies are commenced by ordinary writ issued in the plaintiff's own name. Little wonder that there was and still remains a preference for applicants to use this procedure.

O' Reilly v Mackman

In the important decision of the House of Lords in *O'Reilly v Mackman* (1983) it was, however, held to be an abuse of the process of court to allow an action to continue by way of writ when it should rightly have been commenced under the Order 53 procedure with all its constraints.

Lord Diplock concluded that the reasons justifying the avoidance of Order 53 had now been removed with the procedural reforms of 1977 and there were sound policy reasons justifying the insistence that an applicant overcome the Order 53 safeguards.

Nevertheless, Lord Diplock recognised that there would be exceptions to this general rule:

> ... particularly where the invalidity of the decision arises as a collateral issue in a claim ... under private law, or where none of the parties objects to ... procedure by writ.

Roy v Kensington, Chelsea and Westminster FPC

The severity of this general rule became the cause of much academic debate and in *Roy v Kensington, Chelsea and Westminster Family Practitioner Committee* (1992) Lord Lowry set about defusing the 'procedural minefield' laid by Lord Diplock. With the support of his colleague Lord Bridge, he made clear that in his view *O'Reilly v Mackman* (1983) should be given a limited interpretation, so as not to create a general rule that all challenges to public law decisions had to follow the Order 53 procedure, subject to exceptional cases involving private law rights.

He set out four main reasons why Dr Roy's challenge for repayment of money due should not be struck out as an abuse of the process of court simply because it was commenced by writ. First, he was seeking to protect private law rights. Second, those rights dominated the proceedings. Third, the remedy he sought could not be obtained under Order 53 and lastly it was inappropriate to require Dr Roy to use Order 53 to claim a non-discretionary remedy.

In his article, 'Private Rights and Public Procedure' (1992) *Public Law*, Peter Cane considers each of these four reasons and concludes that the last two do not bear up to closer examination. He can see no reason why Dr Roy should not have used the Order 53 procedure to claim a non-discretionary remedy. Likewise, Ord 53 r 7 allows for the 'award of damages', which in his view is sufficiently broad to cover the repayment of money due. He cites *Woolwich Equitable v IRC* (1991) and the limitations of s 31(4) of the Supreme Court Act 1981 but argues that, 'there is no good reason why ... (its) effects should not be extended to cover any monetary remedy ...'.

The strength of Lord Lowry's argument therefore lies in the first two reasons. Together with his judicial colleagues in the House of Lords he treated Dr Roy as having private law statutory rights. Thus the question has now become which statutory duties give rise to rights enforceable in private law, the private rights test?

This was the approach adopted by Judges in the Court of Appeal decision of *Lonrho v Tebbit* (1992). In dismissing the appeal Lord Justices Dillon, Kerr and Stocker held that whereas *Rowling v Takaro Properties* (1988) presented a significant hurdle to establishing a private law duty owed by a Secretary of State acting in the public interest, the suggestion was not untenable in law. Therefore the action should not be struck out for having been commenced by writ, since Lonrho was trying to assert a private law right against a public law background.

The need for further reform

Crown Office list

All public law procedures are processed through a single office in the High Court known as the Crown Office, situated in room 126. Cases from the Crown Office list are divided into five parts, Part A – cases ready to be heard, Part B – cases not ready to be heard, Part C – cases stood out, Part D – the expedited list and Part E – cases listed for hearing. Almost all the cases are heard by specially assigned High Court Judges, known as 'nominated Judges', chosen by the Lord Chief Justice on the basis of their expertise in administrative law.

However, in an article entitled 'Public Law in the High Court' (1991) *Legal Executive*, Richard Gordon notes that whereas 'many practitioners, when confronted with a public law problem, think only of judicial review', there are in fact a number of, 'very important procedures which need to be considered alongside Order 53 ...'. In particular, case stated appeals, *habeas corpus* applications, statutory appeals to the High Court and statutory review.

Justice/All Souls

In the 1960s a series of seminars were held in All Souls College, Oxford by the Law Commission to investigate procedural and other defects in our public law. The Law Commission recommended the establishment of a Royal Commission to investigate the matter. The failure of successive governments to take action ultimately led to the formation of an unofficial body of investigation. To quote from its report, 'in 1978 a Committee was formed under the auspices of JUSTICE (the British section of the International Commission of Jurists) and All Souls College, Oxford, to undertake a full scale examination of administrative law in the United Kingdom'.

It was against this background of an on-going review that the Law Commission made its Report, 'Remedies in Administrative Law' (1976) which led to the reform of Order 53 in 1977 and the passing of s 31 of the Supreme Court Act 1981. In his important contribution to the debate, 'Judicial Review: A Possible Programme For Reform' (1992) *Public Law* the then Sir Harry Woolf expressed his deep concern as to the state and future of judicial review. Such progress as there had been in the 1980s, 'was only possible because of the procedural reforms (cited above) ... they provided a structure within which the developments could take place'.

Lord Woolf continued with his theme by stating:

> The former Lord Chief Justice (Lord Lane) has compared that structure with a motorway and pointed out that, if you provide a motorway, it will become an invitation for the public to respond by using it. This, in the case of judicial review, has proved all too true. There is a danger of it becoming as overcrowded as the M25. The tailback, or backlogs, are becoming more and more disturbing. The use of judicial review has grown and is continuing to grow at a pace with which the present structure cannot cope ... What is more, I believe that the rate of increase, far from slowing down, is going to accelerate.

Public law project

In a unique research project conducted by Maurice Sunkin, Lee Bridges and George Meszaros, a detailed analysis has been made of all applications for judicial review between 1987 to the early part of 1991. In total they analysed nearly 5,000 applications and their findings are summarised in an article entitled, 'The Lottery of Judicial Review' (1993) *Counsel*. These findings are deserving of our attention because they challenge a number of the current assumptions about judicial review.

Underdeveloped

Much has been made by Lord Woolf about the 'explosion' in judicial review applications, yet the research analysis reveals that this expansion has been confined to but three areas namely immigration, housing (homelessness) and criminal proceedings. These three areas consistently account for over 50% of the applications. Indeed, with the exception of town and country planning and education no other area accounted for more than 5% of the applications. This leads us to the conclusion that for a very wide range of government activities the potential for judicial review in fact remains underdeveloped.

Weapon against local not central government

Another striking finding of the research is that judicial review is being used, 'more often as a weapon to limit ... local government than as a constraint on the power of the central State'. Only 25% of the applications were directed against central government and of these 75% were directed against the Home Office, with only five other departments being challenged 10 times or more during the research period.

Applicants

Of the people bringing applications most were instituted in the names of individuals, with a surprisingly low level of litigation instituted in the names of pressure groups. The largest non-individual applications came from companies. Yet concern was expressed by the research team that:

> Access to judicial review is a more serious problem than is generally supposed. The problems arise not only from the limited availability of legal aid but also from the availability of expert legal advice in the field ... only a small minority of private solicitors are likely to have experience of processing a judicial review case.

Final hearings

'Survival' rates for actions were small with only a third likely to reach the final hearing, although the rate varied considerably between subject areas, eg only 11% of immigration applications reached final hearing. Of those that did reach the final hearing there was a one in six chance of getting a ruling against the body challenged. The main reasons for the low survival rates were difficulties in overcoming the leave hurdle and a large number of withdrawals.

Leave

In statistical terms the leave hurdle has become a more demanding obstacle to overcome. During the period 1971–75 leave was granted to 66% of applications. In the early 1980s it had increased to 73%. But during the period of the research the rate had dropped as low as 46% with evidence of Judges using resource 'managerial' criteria for granting or refusing leave. Again the rate varied considerably between subject areas with only a third of immigration applications getting leave compared to a success rate of 80% for homeless applications.

One of the major findings of the research, however, related to:

> ... very wide variations in leave grant rates as between individual Judges ... in the 1987 sample, Judge A (the most liberal Judge) granted leave to 82% of his cases whereas the least liberal, Judge O granted leave in only 21% of his cases.

The research team expected to find some variation in the pattern of individual Judges if only because there were no stated criteria for the granting of leave but, 'the sheer scale of the variation revealed (was) ... surprising ... Some Judges appear to view the leave hurdle as substantially more of a test than do others. The result for the applicants is that leave is something of a lottery'.

Giving reasons

In their report, 'Judicial Review in Perspective: An Investigation of Trends in the Use and Operation of the Judicial Review Procedure in England and Wales' (1993) *Public Law Project*, the research team, whilst acknowledging the need to make the criteria for granting leave more transparent, rejected the idea of a need to 'tighten-up' on leave. They propose instead a different strategy for reform, making the, 'reasons for decisions by public authorities ... available to applicants, their legal advisers and Judges at a much earlier stage'.

The general giving of reasons is a consistent theme in discussions on the reform of administrative law. Lord Woolf wrote in, 'Protection of the Public' (1990) that:

> If I were asked to identify the most beneficial improvement which could be made to English administrative law I would unhesitatingly reply that it would be the introduction of a general requirement that reasons should normally be available, at least on request, for all administrative actions.

Yet there is still no such general duty today. Instead we have a piecemeal system of a statutory duty to provide reasons, such as s 10 of the Tribunals and Inquiries Act 1992 which applies to nearly all tribunals and ministerial decisions after the holding of a Public Inquiry. But in his article, 'Tell Us Why' (1994) *Solicitors Journal*, Professor Anthony Bradley considers that such a general duty is in the process of emerging. In particular, he cites the judgment of Sir Louis Blom-Cooper in *R v Lambeth LBC, ex p Walters* (1993) and his conclusion (following the dicta of Judges of the Court of Appeal in *R v Civil Service Appeal Board, ex p Cunningham* (1991) and Law Lords in *Doody v Home Secretary* (1993)) that, 'the movement towards establishing such a general duty is undeniable'. The rationale for imposing a duty on a decision-maker to give reasons was considered in *R v Higher Education Funding Council, ex p Dental Surgery* (1994).

In *R v Secretary of State for the Home Department, ex p Moon* (1995), it was held that the failure of the Secretary of State to explain his reasons for concluding that the entry into the UK of the Reverend Sun Myung Moon would not be conducive to the public good was unfair and contrary to the rules of natural justice. But in *R v Secretary of State for the Home Department, ex p Al-Fayed* (1996), the Divisional Court ruled that there was no duty to give reasons for refusing applications for naturalisation under s 44(2) of the British Nationality Act 1981. On appeal, however, the Court of Appeal quashed the Home Secretary's decision on the basis that he did have a duty to indicate to an applicant the area(s) of concern on which he was basing his refusal, in order that the applicant might have an opportunity to allay concerns.

Withdrawals

On the issue of withdrawals of applications for judicial review it was found that between 31%–42% of all applications over the research period were withdrawn. The majority of withdrawals had taken place after leave had been granted. The implication of the research finding, 'is that respondents may be shielding behind the leave requirement and only seriously considering a settlement once leave had been obtained'. It is interesting to note in this regard that during the early 1991 period over 60% of homelessness applications were withdrawn prior to reaching a substantive hearing.

Law Commission

Proposals for further procedural reform have been considered by the Law Commission in its most recent paper *Administrative Law: Judicial Review and Statutory Appeals* (1994). Whereas media attention has tended to focus on the recommendation to simplify the title of the remedies from *mandamus*, prohibition and *certiorari* and to mandatory, restraining and quashing orders, it is the areas of leave and *locus standi* (standing) which contain the most interesting proposals. The Law Commission would recommend re-naming leave 'preliminary consideration' and suggests a test whereby the applicant discloses 'a serious issue', rather than the present test of showing 'an arguable case'. Judges would make a 'request for information' from respondents and would be required to give reasons for refusing leave. The area of *locus standi* has already undergone considerable development, from the reluctance of judges to allow a public interest challenge in *R v Secretary of State for the Environment, ex p Rose Theatre Trust* (1990), to allowing standing for Greenpeace in *R v Inspectorate of Pollution, ex p Greenpeace* (1994), the Equal Opportunities Commission in *R v Secretary of State for Employment, ex p Equal Opportunities Commission* (1994) and the World Development Movement in *R v Secretary of State for Foreign and Commonwealth Affairs, ex p World Development Movement* (1994). The Law Commission would envisage a two-track system of standing in judicial review proceedings. Individual applicants with 'legal personality' would continue to have standing, but only in matters where they have been 'personally adversely affected' by the decision. In public interest challenges the Law Commission would recommend a 'broad discretion' as to standing, and a corresponding amendment to s 31(4)(b) of the Supreme Court Act 1981.

Professor Richard Gordon would note that, 'case load management philosophy looms large in the Commission's proposals, especially in respect of the leave stage. So, too, does the creation of a new public interest focus. The two philosophies are not necessarily mutually exclusive but they are hardly complimentary'.

Grounds for judicial review

Old grounds

Up until 1984 the textbooks traditionally defined the grounds for judicial review as being *ultra vires* caused by the breach of a rule of natural justice, or caused by the failure to follow a procedural requirement prescribed by statute, or caused by a body acting in excess of its legal jurisdiction or abusing its powers by acting in contravention of the 'Wednesbury principles'. The only exception was a ground for review, revived in *R v Northumberland Compensation Appeal Tribunal, ex p Shaw* (1952) of 'error of law on the face of the record'. This was an exception because the body was acting within its jurisdiction when taking the decision (ie *intra vires*) but the decision had been reached via an erroneous interpretation of the law recorded in its proceedings.

New classification

The categorisation of the grounds of review changed, however, with the judgment of Lord Diplock in the leading case of *Council of Civil Service Unions v Minister for the Civil Service* (1985):

> Judicial review has I think developed to a stage today when without reiterating any analysis of the steps by which the development has come about, one can conveniently classify under three heads the grounds upon which administrative action is subject to control by judicial review. The first ground I would call 'illegality', the second 'irrationality' and the third 'procedural impropriety'. That is not to say that further development on a case by case basis may not in the course of time add further grounds ... By 'illegality' as a ground for judicial review I mean that the decision-maker must understand correctly the law that regulates his decision-making power and must give effect to it. Whether he has or not is *par excellence* a justiciable question to be decided, in the event of dispute, by those persons, the Judges, by whom the judicial power of state is exercisable. By 'irrationality' I mean what can by now be succinctly referred to as 'Wednesbury unreasonableness'... It applies to a decision which is so outrageous in its defiance of logic or of accepted moral standards that no sensible person who had applied his mind to the question to be decided could have arrived at it ... I have described the third head as 'procedural impropriety' rather than failure to observe basic rules of natural justice ... because ... this head covers failure by an administrative tribunal to observe procedural rules that are expressly laid down in the leg-

islative instrument by which its jurisdiction is conferred, even where such failure does not involve any denial of natural justice.

Two stages

The categorisation of the grounds for judicial review is important for the undergraduate constitutional law student because it provides a useful checklist to apply to the problem scenario in the examination. In her article, 'Is the *Ultra Vires* Rule the Basis of Judicial Review? (1987) *Public Law*, Professor Dawn Oliver reached the conclusion that when exercising their supervisory jurisdiction Judges first concern themselves with the question of whether the decision-maker was acting within their *vires* (illegality). If the answer to this question is in the affirmative, then the Judges turn to the next question of whether it can be made out that the decision-maker was abusing their power (procedural impropriety and irrationality).

Mistake of fact

What you are required to look for is a mistake on the part of the decision-maker which causes his decision to be derived from illegality, procedural impropriety and irrationality. A problem arises here in that there can be mistakes of fact or mistakes of law. Appeal mechanisms are distinct from judicial review in that the appeal Judge is able to address the quality of the decision made as opposed to the way in which the decision, good or bad, was reached. Thus one might think that mistakes of fact are better left to considerations of an appeal.

However, consider the situation of a statute setting up a rent review tribunal (from whose decisions there may be no right of appeal) which has the power to prescribe a level of fair rent for furnished accommodation. The jurisdiction of the decision-making body is limited to 'furnished accommodation'. But if there is a dispute as to whether, as a matter of objective fact, the accommodation is 'furnished' or 'unfurnished' does one leave it to the tribunal to decide upon the issue unsupervised by the Judges?

Surely not, for if the matter were to be left exclusively to the tribunal it could, through its powers of interpretation of objective fact, give itself excessive or unlimited jurisdiction. This is why Lord Diplock referred to such issues as being *par excellence* justicable (ie capable of review by the Judge).

It is for this reason that we must distinguish between mistakes of fact going to the jurisdiction, known as mistakes of jurisdictional fact (capable of review), and mistakes of fact not going to the jurisdiction, known as mistakes of non-jurisdictional fact. It would appear that a Judge will not hold a non-jurisdictional mistake capable of review (unless the error is so excessive as to render the decision unreasonable or that there is no or insufficient evidence of the existence of facts which are required to exist before the decision can be made).

Mistake of law

But how does one distinguish between a mistake of law and a mistake of fact. In his article, 'Mistake of Fact in Administrative Law' (1990) *Public Law*, Timothy Jones states that, 'in simple terms one can say that a fact is a quality or event occurring at a definite place and time ... In contrast, "[l]aw is expressed in distinctive propositions"' (Hall, *General Principles of Criminal Law* (1960)). Thus, 'that A has killed P is a fact; the conclusion that this constitutes the crime of murder (rather than being, say, an accidental or justifiable killing) can be reached only through the application of certain propositions of law'. But as Timothy Jones notes whereas, 'analytical and conceptual distinctions can be drawn between fact and law in practice, boundary disputes attend any attempt to draw a rigorous distinction ...'.

Once it has been decided that the error is indeed a mistake of law, then *Anisminic v Foreign Compensation Commission* (1969) would lead us to conclude that all errors of law, will invalidate the decision. If we recognise that all mistakes of law are jurisdictional then error of law on the face of the record as a grounds for judicial review becomes redundant.

Illegality

For illegality to exist as a grounds for judicial review the applicant will need to convince the Judge of:

- Misinterpretation
  That the decision-maker misinterpreted the statute (which gave the decision-making power) to the extent that the decision-maker had acted, 'outside the four corners of the statute' and has done something they simply do not have the power to do.
- Improper purpose
  That the decision-maker used the decision-making power for a purpose not specified or implied in the statute.
- Relevant/irrelevant considerations
  That the decision-maker in reaching the decision failed to take into

account a relevant consideration and/or took into account an irrelevant consideration. Since there are very few cases where a mistake of fact has in itself given rise to a judicial review it is suggested that the applicant would be better advised to try and use the mistake in this third category and thereby establish illegality.

- Failure to retain a discretion
The decision-maker fails to retain a discretion in the exercise of a power by delegating the decision-making power to some other body not prescribed by Parliament or by identifying in advance how the discretionary power is to be exercised and then over-rigidly adhering to the application of that policy.

Procedural impropriety

Lord Diplock's second ground for review, procedural impropriety, is established by convincing the Judge that there has been a breach of a rule of natural justice, failure on the part of the decision-maker to follow correct procedures or the breach of a legitimate expectation.

- Natural justice
The three rules of natural justice are *audi alteram partem* (no man to be condemned without a hearing), *nemo judex in causa sua* (no man to be Judge in his own cause) and a general duty for decision-makers to act fairly (although the existence of this duty is sometimes called into question).
- Failure to adhere to procedural requirements
The decision-maker fails to observe a procedural requirement expressly stated in the statute conferring the decision-making power. Whereas the object of these specific requirements may always be considered as being mandatory (imperative), Judges have allowed themselves the flexibility of regarding some express requirements as being merely directory.
- Legitimate expectation
Applicants may legitimately expect a decision-maker to act in a specific way by either an express promise or regular past practice. Whereas natural justice will only give rise to procedural impropriety if the applicant's interests are sufficiently affected, with legitimate expectation the Judge has only to decide upon its existence and then the appropriate remedy for a breach. However, the appropriate remedy will often turn upon the adverse effects of the breach on the applicant.

Irrationality

Prior to Lord Diplock's third classification of 'irrationality', this ground for review used to be referred to as 'Wednesbury unreasonableness'. Judges created a fiction by saying that in giving a power to a decision-maker Parliament would never expect the decision-maker to use the power unreasonably. Thus if a decision-maker were to use its discretionary powers unreasonably that would be acting *ultra vires* and therefore subject to judicial review. But it is inappropriate to talk of *ultra vires* when the decision-maker is using a prerogative power. So Judges now claim an inherent jurisdiction to supervise decision-makers acting in abuse of their power.

Wednesbury unreasonableness means that the decision-maker reached a decision that no rational decision-maker would have made. Thus Lord Diplock re-classified the ground and called it 'irrationality'. Subsequent cases, however, have reflected a reluctance on the part of Judges to call decisions 'irrational' given the emotive response it provokes in the decision-maker. But attempts to refer to this head as 'perversity' have equally met with little success. Whatever its title it does exist as a ground for judicial review, although it has to be said that an applicant is unlikely to achieve success using this ground alone.

New grounds?

In identifying the three grounds of illegality, procedural impropriety and irrationality it is clear that inevitable overlaps may exist. Moreover, Lord Diplock left open the possibility of the development of new grounds. In particular, he identified the concept of 'proportionality' as a possible fourth ground for judicial review. However, in *R v Home Office, ex p Brind* (1991) the majority of Judges in the House of Lords were not prepared to extend their powers of review to challenge the proportionality of the Minister's directives to the mischief at which they were aimed. It was suggested instead that proportionality was but part of 'Wednesbury unreasonableness' and not a separate head of challenge.

Yet proportionality is clearly a separate principle of review under Community law and therefore already presents a separate head for cases in the UK with a 'European element'. Just as it is illogical to allow interim relief against the Crown only for Community law matters so it is illogical to allow proportionality as a separate ground of review only for Community law matters. For many commentators it is simply a matter of time before proportionality is accepted as a fourth ground of judicial review.

Public Interest Immunity Certificates

Discovery

It is an established principle of litigation that prior to trial each party has access to all the evidence which is to be used in the trial. This procedure is known as discovery. However, when one of the parties to the action happens to be the Crown, special rules apply to enable the Judge to order that documents should not be used where disclosure would be contrary to the public interest.

Known up until 1975 as 'Crown privilege', public interest immunity (PII) has developed principally through a series a civil cases. A claim to immunity from discovery can be based either upon the content of the particular document in question or the fact that it belongs to a protected class of document.

In *Duncan v Cammell Laird* (1942) a tort action involving the death of sailors (when the submarine *Thetis* sank) in sea trials in Liverpool Bay was thwarted when the Admiralty issued a PII certificate against disclosure of the plans used in building the submarine. In *Conway v Rimmer* (1968) Judges were ready to recognise that public interest in preventing the disclosure of documents had also to be balanced against public interest in the administration of justice. Thus Judges decided to involve themselves in adjudicating upon whether discovery should be permitted. The issuing of the certificate was, therefore, no longer to be treated as being conclusive. However, in *Air Canada v Secretary of State for Trade* (1983) Judges in the House of Lords decided by majority that a decision by the Judge to inspect the contested documents would be limited to instances where it is reasonably likely that the documents would assist the party seeking discovery or damage the party opposing disclosure.

Matrix Churchill

Recent interest in claims of public interest immunity have heightened with the criminal trial of Paul Henderson, Trevor Abraham and Peter Allan, three directors of Matrix Churchill, a company which manufactured and exported machine tools to Iraq. Four Ministers signed PII certificates in relation to the trial: Tristan Garel-Jones (Foreign Office Minister), Malcolm Rifkind (Secretary of State for Defence), Michael Heseltine (President of the Board of Trade) and Kenneth Clarke (as Home Secretary).

The documents to which the certificates related were: Category A – information from a confidential informant, Category B – Ministerial and departmental documents and Category C – documents relating to security and intelligence matters. Justice Smedley decided to inspect all three categories of documents. He agreed that Category A should not be disclosed, 'save in the most exceptional circumstances'. He did not order discovery for he felt upon inspection that the documents would be of no assistance to the defence. However, disclosure was ordered of Category B documents, even those documents not specifically mentioning Matrix Churchill. Originally Category C documents were not disclosed as the defence had failed to discharge the burden raised in the strongly worded certificates. Nevertheless, the strength of the defence claim, that both the government and the security services knew of the use being made of the machine tools, eventually warranted their disclosure during the course of the trial.

Scott Inquiry

The collapse of the trial, after the evidence of former Minister Alan Clarke demonstrated the validity of this defence, provoked a political outcry. Responding to this, the Prime Minister, John Major, set up the Scott Inquiry.

While media analysis of the Scott Report has focused on the political implications, its significance for the constitutional law student lies more in the examination of the law on public interest immunity. In an article entitled, 'The Law According to Scott' (1996) *Solicitors Journal*, Charles Foster and Nicholas Ainsley consider Sir Richard Scott's conclusion that the Attorney-General, Sir Nicholas Lyell, was labouring under a misconception when he failed to draw any, or any sufficient, distinction between the application of PII in civil and criminal proceedings.

The Attorney-General relied on the remarks of the then Lord Justice Bingham in *Makanjuola v Commissioner of Police of the Metropolis* (1992) to justify his assertion that immunity had to be asserted where documents were in a class which was *prima facie* immune from disclosure. In the view of Sir Richard Scott, this was taking the remarks beyond the presumed intentions of their maker. The conclusion of the Scott Report is that whereas the judgment of Lord Templeman in *R v Chief Constable of the West Midlands Police, ex p Wiley* (1994) provides the basic guidance as to whether a PII claim should be made in either a civil or criminal case, different considerations will apply to criminal proceedings. Lord Taylor CJ in *R v Keane* (1994) argued that if disputed material 'may prove the defendant's innocence or avoid a miscarriage of justice then the balance (of public interests) comes down resoundingly in favour of disclosing it'.

Foster and Ainley note that Sir Richard would hold that a document which might be of assistance to the defence would always be a document that might prove the defendant's innocence or avoid a miscarriage of justice. If this is an accurate assessment, then claims to PII based solely on class have no place in criminal litigation.

Ouster clauses

'Judge over your shoulder'

The importance of our study of judicial review lies in the fact that it provides one of the few effective mechanisms within our constitution to keep a check on the activities of the executive. Needless to say the executive is not unaware of this fact and has produced a guide for civil servants entitled 'The Judge Over Your Shoulder', *Judicial Review: Balancing Scales* (1994), which warns of the dangers of judicial review.

It is not unknown for the executive to use its dominance of the legislature to try to limit or exclude the power of judicial review by inserting ouster clauses into legislation. Ouster clauses are so called for they attempt to 'oust' the jurisdiction of the Judge to grant the remedy of a prerogative order against the decision-maker. These clauses are 'total' or 'partial' (eg six-week time constraint) in their effect. Judges tend to be hostile in their interpretation of the former and tolerant of the latter.

'Total' ouster clauses

The differing varieties of ouster clauses which have 'total' effect have successfully been circumvented by Judges. A good example of this would be the decision of Judges in the House of Lords *in Anisminic v Foreign Compensation Commission* (1969). A clause in the relevant legislation held that decisions of the Commission, 'shall not be called into question in any court of law'. Using their powers of statutory interpretation the Judges interpreted this clause as only applying to a decision made within the Commission's jurisdiction. If there had been no jurisdiction to make a decision then the clause had no effect.

Judges later went on to suggest that the effect of *Anisminic v Foreign Compensation Commission* (1969) was to hold that all errors of law inevitably went to the decision-makers' jurisdiction. Evidence for this can be seen in the judgment of Lord Denning MR in *Pearlman v Keepers and Governors of Harrow School* (1979). But in *Re Racal Communications* (1981) Judges sought a compromise solution by merely holding that a presumption existed, when a statute conferred a decision-making power, that the decision-maker was not intended to be the final arbiter on questions of law.

Non-statutory power

But what of a decision-maker using a power not conferred by statute? In *R v Hull University Visitor, ex p Page* (1992) it was held that whereas *mandamus* would lie to compel a Visitor to adjudicate on a disciplinary matter and prohibition would restrain the Visitor from acting outside their jurisdiction, certiorari would not be used for a mere error on the part of a University Visitor.

In an article critical of the judgment entitled, 'Visitors and Error of Law' (1993) *Law Quarterly Review*, Professor Sir William Wade, whilst acknowledging that error of law on the face of the record, 'can deservedly be consigned to oblivion', and that, 'the same fate has over-taken the distinction between jurisdictional and non-jurisdictional (mistakes of) law', could see little logic in applying an exception to the latter in the case of Visitors.

The justification cited by Lord Browne-Wilkinson, upholding the judgment of Lord Holt CJ in *Philips v Bury* (1694), was that an eleemosynary corporation is governed by a system of private law which is not of 'the common known laws of the kingdom' but is pre-scribed by the founder. This is considered by Professor Sir William Wade to be unconvincing, 'for there would seem to be no reason why the courts should not interpret university and college charters and statutes as readily as they interpret private wills, settlements and con-tracts'.

5 The citizen and the State

You should be familiar with the following areas:

- civil liberties and issues of national security
- freedom of association and assembly
- freedom of expression
- freedom of the person and police powers
- Bill of Rights debate

Introduction

Constitutional law is a foundation subject in any study of law at undergraduate level. There are, however, three areas of the syllabus for which, in many LLB programmes, it provides a basic introduction for further study in later years. These areas may be identified as European law, administrative law and civil liberties.

In Chapter 1 we noted that for the purpose of studying issues of constitutional law we need to be aware of the European Union, Community institutions, Community laws and their effect on our traditional doctrine of parliamentary sovereignty. In Chapter 4 we recognised the importance of judicial review as a mechanism which allows for our judges to keep a check on the activities of the executive.

In this chapter we are called upon to study the body of law which regulates a citizen's liberties and freedoms within our State. This is a specialist area of law which is often covered in specific textbooks. However, for the purpose of our study we need only address the constitutional issue of the degree to which a balance is struck between legal protection of the interests of the individual citizen and the protection of the State.

Distinguishing between rights and liberties

Liberal theory of rights

In the view of John Locke, a civilised State is founded upon a social contract between the State and its citizens, whereby the citizens for the protection of their property hand over powers to their government, such as a monopoly of coercive force, in return for the guarantee of certain rights. John Rawls developed this idea further by specifying that 'the first principle' in this social contract is a total system of equal basic liberties for all. In his work Ronald Dworkin concentrated on the need to protect the 'unpopular' rights of minorities within a State. In particular, he identified 'trump' rights which, whatever the popular view within the State, needed to be protected to preserve basic human dignity.

Nevertheless, situations may arise which require the limitation of citizens' rights within a State. In the first instance the rights of two individual citizens within a State may come into conflict, such as A using his freedom of expression to incite racial hatred against a group to which B is a member. Alternatively, a claim by A to freedom of expression may be diluted by the purpose for which the claim is made, eg selling hard-core pornography for commercial gain. Caution might also be exercised where the exercise of an individual right poses a real danger to the State, such as a civil servant claiming freedom of expression to leak sensitive information to the media.

Holfeld

From a constitutional perspective there is an important distinction between giving the citizens within a State legally enforceable rights, as opposed to offering the legal protection of citizens' liberties. It is here that we need to look at the work of the American jurist *Professor Wesley Holfeld* who broke down claims into four main sections:

Claim right

A 'claim right' is where C claims a right and persons, generally or specifically, are under a corresponding duty to allow C access to that right.

Immunity claim

An 'immunity' claim is where C, exercises a right and persons, generally or specifically, are under a duty not to interfere in the exercise of that right.

Power claim

A 'power' claim is where C has a right of ownership which can be exercised to create a liability. Thus C may offer to sell the ownership rights in goods to B and thereby creates a liability.

Privilege claim

A 'privilege' claim merely means that C has done no wrong in exercising his liberty to do something. To Holfeld this is the weakest claim because nobody has a duty to allow or assist C in the exercise of his liberty.

Holfeld's analysis is not without its critics but it is particularly useful for us because it serves to demonstrate the difference in approach between civil rights and civil liberties. Our constitution does not contain a charter giving positive 'claim rights' to particular freedoms. Instead, we leave it to Parliament and our judges to determine on an *ad hoc* basis what legal restrictions on an individual's freedom will and will not be permitted for the protection of the State.

Dicey

What Holfeld would see as a weakness for the UK, Diceyan theorists see as a strength. For Professor A V Dicey it is a fundamental feature of our constitution and its adherence to the concept of the rule of law that the rights of our individual citizens transcend (came before) the constitution. This means that a citizen of the UK has a liberty to do whatever it is they want to do, subject to any restriction placed upon their action in law for the benefit of the State as a whole. For Professor Dicey this concept of residual liberties provides for a better protection of individual freedom than any written charter. The role of the judge, therefore, is to determine on a case by case basis what restrictions the law permits for the benefit of society as a whole.

Balance

Our task is to ascertain whether we have struck the correct constitutional balance between your freedom to do whatever you want and the legal restrictions imposed upon that freedom for the protection of society as a whole. We are required, therefore, to analyse the residual liberties permitted under our constitution in the areas of freedom of association, assembly, expression and freedom of the person.

Your freedom to associate, meet and demonstrate

Association

It is often said, usually in exasperation, that you can choose your friends but you cannot choose your family. Whatever the merits of this saying, we should note that your freedom to choose your friends, people with whom you would wish to associate, is tempered by legal restriction. There are certain categories of people that the State wishes to prevent you from associating with, for the better running of society in general.

Quasi-military organisations

Under the Public Order Act 1936 and the Prevention of Terrorism (Temporary Provisions) Act 1989 special restrictions apply to associating with quasi-military organisations which have political objectives deemed detrimental to the interests of the State.

Thus *R v Jordan and Tyndall* (1963) saw the successful prosecution of two members of the fascist group Spearhead, deemed a prohibited group to associate with, in accordance with the Public Order Act 1936 s 2(1)b. In *McEldowney v Forde* (1971) an extensive prohibition on association with republican clubs or any like organisation was upheld by judges in the House of Lords.

Political neutrality

In accordance with the concept of the separation of powers members of the armed forces, police, senior civil servants and judges are prohibited from active association with political groups. Political instability within a State can often arise if the military is actively involved in State politics. The dangers of a *coup* are obviously heightened.

Employment

Issues relating to your freedom of association can also arise within the context of work. We have already seen in *Council for Civil Service Unions v Minister for the Civil Service* (1985) that staff at GCHQ, the sensitive government communications headquarters, were prohibited by Order in Council from any further association with their trade unions.

In *Young, James and Webster v UK* (1981) the opposite problem occurred when employees were dismissed by their employer for not associating with a trade union. British Rail had entered into a closed-shop agreement which was found by the European Court of Human Rights to contravene Article 11 of the European Convention on Human Rights, since it infringed freedom of choice. The resultant change in UK law renders a dismissal unlawful if you have a deeply held conviction against association with trade unions.

Demonstrate

The significance of the freedom to associate lies in the political importance of collective strength. One means of bringing public attention to the validity of a cause is to meet and demonstrate this collective strength. Yet this freedom often falls prey to severe restrictions deemed necessary in light of public disorder problems. For example, statutory restrictions were imposed under the Public Order Act 1936 to combat Fascist marches in the East End of London in the 1930s. The Public Order Act 1986 was deemed necessary to combat the inner city riots of the 1980s and public disorder problems associated with the miners' strike in 1984. Indeed the 1986 Act, and the strengthening by the courts of police common law powers during the 1984 miners' strike, means that our freedom to demonstrate is among the most severely curtailed freedoms in recent times.

Meetings

The problem associated with our freedom to meet usually stems from the issue of where the meeting is supposed to take place. All land is owned by someone and, with few exceptions (see *Webster v Southwark LBC* (1983)), it is for the owners to determine whether they will permit a meeting to be held on their land. Where an owner does permit a meeting to take place on their land *Thomas v Sawkins* (1935) proves that, irrespective of whether it is a private meeting, the police may insist on their being in attendance.

Up until the Public Order Act 1986 there was very little statutory control of public assemblies. The Highways Act 1980 s 137 placed some restriction on meetings obstructing the highway, no matter how trivial the obstruction (see *Arrowsmith v Jenkins* (1963)). However, the Public Order Act 1986 and the Criminal Justice and Public Order Act 1994 now contain provisions which are specific to assemblies and processions – namely, ss 12–15 of the Public Order Act 1986 (as amended by the 1994 Act) and ss 70–71 of the Criminal Justice and Public Order Act 1994.

Other public order offences

In addition, the Public Order Act 1986 also provides for the statutory offences of riot (s 1), violent disorder (s 2), affray (s 3), threatening behaviour (ss 4 and 5) and incitement to racial hatred (s 18), which may also affect freedom of assembly. Complementing these public order offences is the offence of obstructing a police officer under s 51(3) of the Police Act 1964. In *Rice v Connolly* (1966) this offence was held to be committed if a person knowingly or intentionally impedes a police officer in the execution of his or her duty.

Police powers are further enhanced by the common law. For example, a public nuisance may arise from blocking the highway if, as in *R v Clarke* (No 2) (1964), the disruption is caused by an unreasonable user of the highway. The miners' strike of 1984 saw increasing use made of the common law offence of breach of the peace. In *Moss v McLachlan* (1985) police power to regulate and control public assemblies was extended, upon the apprehension of a breach of the peace, not only to stopping vehicles and questioning the occupants but also to requiring that they discontinue their journey.

Moreover, it was affirmed in *R v Home Office, ex p Northumbria Police Authority* (1989) that, irrespective of the wishes of the local police authority, the Crown had a prerogative power to keep the peace which allowed the Home Secretary to, 'do all that was reasonably necessary to preserve the peace of the realm'. In addition, magistrates' also have a power, dating back to Justices of the Peace Act 1361, of binding over a defendant to keep the peace. The Law Commission has recommended reform of this power and there has been much criticism of its use against environmental protesters opposed to motorway developments.

It should be noted that special rules govern picketing in contemplation or furtherance of a trade dispute. Section 220 of the Trade Union and Labour Relations (Consolidation) Act 1992 provides some immunity where the pickets are acting peacefully, as in *Hubbard v Pitt* (1976) and at their own place of work. Such protection is lost, however, if the real intention of the pickets is to merely obstruct or harass others, as in *Thomas v NUM (South Wales)* (1986).

Your freedom to expression

Can you read any article or book you want to read, see any film or play, watch on television that which you want to see, or view any art that appeals to you? The problem lies in the fact that what you may view as indulging in the finer things of life, others may view as being offensive and harmful to the well-being of society. Surely civil liberties are as much about protecting one from the abuses of one's fellow citizens as they are about protecting one from the abuses of the State? So where do we draw the line between freedom of expression and restricting that which is harmfully obscene or indecent?

Censorship

To facilitate our study of this area let us look first at the issue of censorship. At one time plays and opera were an important means of mass communication. But as other means of mass communication developed so regulation of this area ceased to be of major importance. By the late 1950s and early 1960s playwrights such as John Osborne and Harold Pinter were pushing the antiquated system of theatre censorship, via the Lord Chamberlain office, to its limits.

The Theatres Act 1968 was passed to cover live performances of a play or ballet. The Act does allow, subject to the approval of the Attorney-General, for the prosecution of obscene performances. But the reluctance to prosecute under this Act, even when prompted by campaigners such as Mary Whitehouse (see *Romans in Britain* performed by the National Theatre in 1982) means that this is probably one of the least controlled areas of artistic expression. Any live performance not covered by the Theatres Act 1968 still comes within the ambit of the common law and thus the offences of presenting an indecent exhibition and keeping a disorderly house. In *Moores v DPP* (1991) the common law was used to restrict a live performance which involved an 'exotic dancer' having parts of his male anatomy rubbed with oil by a female member of the audience.

Much of the audience that used to go to the theatres for entertainment was lost to a new medium, cinema. Early cinema film was highly combustible and therefore constituted a fire hazard to large audiences confined in a darkened space. To combat this danger the Cinematograph Act 1909 was passed which provided for the licensing of cinemas by local authorities. It was not long, however, before local authorities began using this licensing power to regulate the type of film being shown in the cinema. Thus in 1912 the industry set up a self-censoring body, the British Board of Film Classification (BBFC), which still operates today. An 18 rating given by the Board to a film effectively means that in the opinion of the Board the film would survive a prosecution under the obscene publications legislation. But whatever the view of the BBFC, your local authority may still refuse to grant a licence to show a film in your area under the Cinemas Act 1985 (which together with the Local Government (Miscellaneous Provisions) Act 1982 is used to regulate sex cinemas and other sex establishments). Examples of films given an 18 rating by the BBFC but banned by some local authorities include: *A Clockwork Orange, The Life of Brian, The Last Temptation of Christ* and *Crash*.

In the early 1980s cinema faced competition from the rapidly growing video rental market. Despite the fact that video cassettes were covered by the obscene publications legislation, public concern over regulating the new video market resulted in the passing of the Video Recordings Act 1984 (as amended by the Criminal Justice and Public Order Act 1994), which prohibits the sale or rental of videos not classified by the BBFC. In similar fashion, public concern presently centres on the opportunities available for children to access scenes of violence or sex on their home computer. In response to growing parental concern the computer games industry has just announced a new system of voluntary classification to indicate the level of violence contained within the games.

But whereas we may with a degree of frequency hire a video or go to the cinema and perhaps less frequently attend the theatre to see a play, ballet or opera, we are much more likely to watch television and read the newspapers. These are the two most important means of mass communication today. So what rules of censorship operate in these areas?

The Broadcasting Act 1990 established a new Independent Television Commission (ITC) to replace the Independent Broadcasting Authority (IBA). This body is now charged with licensing and regulating non-BBC television. Under s 6 it must ensure that programmes are both in 'good taste and decency' and politically 'impartial'.

BBC broadcasting is not subject to this statutory restraint but is controlled by a Board of Governors, appointed by the government, which may look into such matters. However, public demonstrations of editorial interference by the Board are rare, if only because they damage the BBC's reputation for independence.

All television broadcasting now also comes under the supervision of a new Broadcasting Standards Council (BSC), which under s 152 of the Broadcasting Act 1990 draws up a code of guidance for broadcasters on how they should portray sex and violence. In addition to monitoring programmes for taste and decency the BSC may also investigate complaints, initiated by itself if required, of programmes which breach these standards. The government's decision to 'de-regulate' our television with the passing of the Broadcasting Act 1990 means that we also have to take into account satellite and cable television. This has presented the government with a problem because programmes may be made and transmitted out of our jurisdiction. In 1992 the government sought to restrict decoding in the UK of the 'adult' satellite channel 'Red Hot Dutch'. The company unsuccessfully tried to challenge the decision as a breach of free trade within the European Community. But whatever the legal outcome of the case, it clearly served to demonstrate a difference in approach between the UK and other Member States on the question of freedom of expression.

At present our press are largely subject to voluntary self-regulation (see the 'D' Notice system). Concern is regularly expressed, however, about whether we have a correct balance between the freedom of the press to report on any matter they feel may interest you, their reader and the need to protect a person's privacy. The Calcutt Committee on Privacy previously recommended in 1990 that a new Press Complaints Commission (set up in 1991) replace the Press Council and that the press be given one last chance to prove that voluntary self-regulation can work. Continuing public unease with some press coverage led Calcutt to conclude in 1993 that we need a statutory procedure for handling complaints.

Civil law restrictions

One of the most important restraints on our press and broadcasting authorities is the fear of a civil action under the tort of defamation (or indeed for criminal libel). It was a fear of this threat which prompted the passing of Article 9 of the Bill of Rights 1689, discussed in Chapter 2. The details of the tort need not be discussed here. However, it is interesting to note the decision of judges in the House of Lords in *Derbyshire CC v Times Newspapers* (1993). It was held, referring to leading US authorities, that local authorities and by inference government departments could not sue in libel. The *ratio decidendi* of the decision is that freedom of speech under common law is so important as to override a right for public bodies to maintain their reputation against improper attack.

The civil law can also be used to suppress information where that information has been acquired in 'breach of confidence'. This has a particular application to memoirs written by public servants which have national security implications, covered later in this chapter.

Criminal offences

In addition to the official secrets referred to above there are other statutory offences against sedition, incitement to disaffection or racial hatred and blasphemy which also have an impact on free speech. However, the most important statutory offences in this context are those relating to obscenity and indecency. Under s 1 of the Obscene Publications Act 1959 an article is obscene if it has an effect, 'such as to tend to deprave and corrupt persons who are likely, having regard to all the circumstances, to read, see or hear the matter ...'.

R v Penguin Books (1961) was one of the first cases under the Obscene Publications Act 1959 and concerned the publication of *Lady Chatterley's Lover* by D H Lawrence. It was decided in this case that whereas the defence could not argue that there was no intention to deprave and corrupt it could, under the Obscene Publications Act 1959, raise the defence of 'public good' in that the article was, 'in the interests of science, literature, art, learning or of other objects of general concern'. Thus the jury should adopt a two stage approach. Did the article deprave and corrupt and if so did its merits outweigh the obscenity? *DPP v Jordan* (1977) demonstrated, however, that it cannot be argued under the Act that 'hard-core' pornography has the merit of psychotherapeutic value for persons of deviant sexuality. On a further point of interpretation it should be noted that this 'deprave and corrupt' test, as used in Obscene Publications Acts and the Theatres Act 1968, is sufficiently wide to cover not only sexual material but also drug-taking (see *Calder v Powell* (1965)) and violence (see *DPP v A & BC Chewing Gum* (1968)).

Nevertheless, however wide the 'deprave and corrupt' test, it is always going to be easier to prove offences relating to 'indecency' under the Protection of Children Act 1978, Indecent Displays (Control) Act 1981 and the Customs and Excise Management Act 1979. Indeed, the difference in approach between 'obscenity' with its 'deprave and corrupt' test and 'indecency' which relates to 'shocking and disgusting' material, which may not necessarily be obscene, can cause problems. In *Conegate v Customs and Excise Commissioners* (1987), which involved the seizure of life-size inflatable rubber sex-dolls, it was held that the seizure was contrary to Community law. For whereas in *R v Henn* (1981) the goods seized were unlawful in the UK under the obscene publication legislation the same could not be said of the goods in the present instant.

In addition to these statutory restraints on freedom of expression, we also need to note two common law offences, conspiracy to corrupt public morals and outraging public decency. The first of these relates to a new offence created by judges in the House of Lords in *Shaw v DPP* (1962). Shaw published a Ladies Directory which gave the names, addresses and type of service offered by prostitutes in London. The creation of a new offence to corrupt public morals was the cause of much academic criticism but in *Knuller v DPP* (1973), which was concerned with the publication of 'contacts' for homosexuals, judges in the House of Lords reaffirmed both the existence of this offence and another common law offence to outrage public decency. Moreover, in *R v Gibson* (1991) the offence of outraging public decency was held to apply to artistic work, notwithstanding that the offence does not permit any defence in consideration of the artistic merit of the work.

In 1979 a Home Office Committee under the chairmanship of *Professor Bernard Williams* published a report on obscenity and film censorship which concluded that such is the state of our law in this area, 'that it is a complicated task even to piece together a statement of what the law is, let alone attempt to wrestle with or resolve the inconsistencies and anomalies'. Few would disagree that this area of our law is in need of reform but many would disagree as to how best to reform the law. It is for this reason that the proposals of the Williams Committee have been shelved.

Contempt

However, one area of our law affecting freedom of expression which has undergone reform is contempt of court. In *A-G v Times Newspapers* (1974) the parents of malformed children sued Distillers, the distributors of a morning-sickness drug called Thalidomide. *The Sunday Times* campaigned on behalf of the parents arguing that the Company could afford a much more generous offer of compensation than that already made. The question presented to the House of Lords was whether this amounted to contempt. The Publisher and Editor of *The Sunday Times* took the matter to the European Commission on Human Rights and it was as a result of criticism of UK contempt laws that the Contempt of Court Act 1981 was passed. Unfortunately, this Act was not a codifying measure and thus it needs to be read in conjunction with rules of contempt under the common law.

The main categories under which one may be held to be in contempt of court today are scandalising the court, contempt in the face of the court or publishing material which prejudices the course of justice. If one is critical of a judge one may, as in *R v New Statesman (Editor), ex p DPP* (1928), be held in contempt of court for undermining public confidence in the judiciary. But as Lord Atkin pointed out in *Ambard v A-G Trinidad and Tobago* (1936):

> Provided that members of the public abstain from imputing improper motives to those taking part in the administration of justice, and are genuinely exercising a right of criticism, and not acting in malice or attempting to impair the administration of justice, they are immune.

In *Morris v Crown Office* (1970) Welsh language campaigners in a public gallery were held to be in contempt in the face of the court by deliberately disrupting the progress of a trial in order to publicise their cause. In *Secretary of State for Defence v Guardian Newspapers* (1985) it was held that under a 10 of the Contempt of Court Act 1981 you need not necessarily be in contempt if you refuse to respond to questions in court if your responses could identify a confidential informant. However, the case involved the leaking of information to the newspaper about the arrival of cruise missiles at the Greenham Common airbase which the government contended raised issues of national security. In accepting this contention our judges gave the government a legal right to insist on the return of the leaked document, which enabled them to identify and then successfully prosecute Sarah Tisdal as the source of the leak.

In *A-G v News Group Newspapers* (1989) *The Sun* newspaper supported, both financially and in print, the private prosecution of a doctor for the alleged rape of a child. Lord Justice Watkins held that the level of emotive reporting incurred a real risk of prejudicing the fairness of the doctor's trial and therefore found the Editor of *The Sun* to be guilty of contempt under the common law. In *A-G v English* (1983) however, it was held that there is no contempt (even if the publication was capable of prejudicing the jury) if the publication was a discussion in good faith, 'on a matter of wide public interest and the risk of prejudice was incidental'.

Other acts which may also interfere with the course of justice and thus be held in contempt include the naming of a person if prohibited (see Sexual Offences (Amendment) Act 1976 – naming a complainant in a rape case) and publishing information knowing it to be the subject of a court injunction in another case (see *A-G v Times Newspapers* (1992)).

Freedom from interference to your person or property

One of the most important freedoms you can enjoy within a State is your personal liberty. This can be demonstrated by the fact that if the State wishes to punish you for a serious wrongful act then it is likely to incarcerate you. Thus the punishment is the denial of personal liberty.

In determining the degree of balance between personal liberty and the criminal justice system three issues need to be considered. We should seek to ensure that the innocent defendant is not convicted. One way of achieving this is simply by not convicting any defendant. This would of course also be unacceptable because another interest of the criminal justice system is to ensure the conviction of the guilty. Both of these factors have also to be considered in the light of economic use of resources.

The last decade, however, has seen a spate of miscarriages of justice, citizens whose personal liberty have been wrongfully denied by the State. In response to growing public concern a Royal Commission was set up and reported in 1981 on inadequacies in criminal procedures for the safeguarding of suspects. At the time there were no clear powers for the police to stop, search and arrest suspects or enter into premises. Thus the Police and Criminal Evidence Act (PACE) 1984 was introduced with the purpose of putting police powers on a clear statutory footing and at the same time providing greater procedural safeguards for suspects.

Rules are made under the Act which constrain the police in the operation of their formidable powers. In addition to these rules there are *Codes of Practice* made under the Act (revised in 1991) – Code A: stop and search procedures, Code B: searching of premises, Code C: detention and interviewing, Code D: identification and Code E: tape recording. Contained within the Codes of Practice are separate Notes for Guidance. There are numerous Home Office Circulars, some for use with PACE, others which are free standing which also need to be taken into account. Section 67(10) of the PACE 1984 draws a clear distinction between the Act and its Codes in holding that no civil or criminal liability will arise in respect of the breach of a Code. Likewise Notes for Guidance, which assist decisions on the admissibility of evidence and Home Office Circulars, which regulate the relationship between the police and the Home Office, do not provide grounds establishing liability when breached.

It should be noted here that whereas the aforementioned has a general application there is a special class of suspect for which differing rules may apply. Due to the seriousness of the threat to the State the Prevention of Terrorism (Temporary Provisions) Act 1989 (PTA), as amended by ss 81–83 of the Criminal Justice and Public Order Act 1994 often makes special provisions for the terrorist suspect. (See also the Prevention of Terrorism (Additional Powers) Act 1996 referred to later in this chapter.)

Stop and search

So what balance has been struck between protecting your personal liberty and allowing a law enforcement officer of the State to stop you in the street and search you and your vehicle? A legal power to stop and search you is contained in a number of statutes, such as the Misuse of Drugs Act 1971, Sporting Events (Control of Alcohol) Act 1985, Road Traffic Act 1988 and the Criminal Justice and Public Order Act 1994 etc. However, if we confine ourselves to PACE 1984 then under s 1 a police officer has such a power if there is 'reasonable suspicion' (to be assessed to an objective standard by the judge) that stolen goods, offensive weapons or other prohibited articles may be found. Your safeguards as a suspect lie in the fact that this power will have been used unlawfully if the officer failed to follow the procedural requirements of ss 2 and 3 (Code A). Thus before the search the officer must give you, 'his name and the name of the police station to which he is attached, the object of the proposed search, the constable's grounds for proposing to make it'. In addition, the officer must make a record of the search on the spot or as soon as practicable to which you should have access.

Arrest

Being stopped and then searched is one thing, but what is the position if a police officer then seeks to arrest you? The State gives a police officer a power to arrest you either with or without an arrest warrant. A warrant for your arrest may be issued by a magistrate under s 1 of the Magistrates Courts Act 1980. The police officer may also arrest you under ss 24 and 25 of the PACE 1984 without the need for a warrant (see also the Offensive Weapons Act 1996). Section 24 is used for serious offences and may be used where the officer has reasonable grounds to suspect that one of the offences covered by the section is being, is about to be or has been committed. In similar fashion s 25 covers other offences if specific conditions, 'the general arrest conditions', exist. Your safeguards as a suspect lie in the fact that a power to arrest must exist and the procedural requirements of s 28 of the PACE 1984 must be adhered to. Thus you must be informed of your arrest and the reasons for it at the time or as soon as practicable. This will also apply to other statutory powers of arrest without warrant, such as ss 12 and 14 of the Public Order Act 1986. At common law the power to arrest for breach of the peace is unaffected by PACE 1984.

Under s 117 of the PACE 1984 the officer may use reasonable force to arrest you in order to effect a valid arrest. You may be reassured that firearms will only be used to effect your arrest as a last resort. No firearms, according to Home Office Guidelines, should even be issued unless there is reason to suppose that the person to be apprehended is so dangerous that he could not safely be otherwise restrained. The present status of our generally unarmed police force, however, is currently a matter for debate. Certainly the view of officers of the Police Federation is that an armed police force will be required for the effective policing of our State in the next century.

Entry, search and seizure

Has a police officer the legal power to demand entry into your home and search it? We have previously noted a common law power, associated with a breach of the peace, to enter premises. Under s 17 of the PACE 1984 a power exists to enter your home to arrest you, although *McLeod v Metropolitan Police Commissioner* (1994) would imply that caution must be exercised when using this power. Under s 18 of the PACE 1984, immediately after an arrest, an officer can, if there are reasonable grounds for suspecting that evidence exists in connection with the arrest which is not protected by legal privilege, search your premises. A power exists under the foregoing section and s 19 of the PACE 1984 for the officer to seize your goods if there are reasonable grounds for believing they have been obtained in consequence of an offence or that they are evidence of an offence which it is necessary to seize in order to prevent their concealment, adjustment, loss or destruction. Under Code B, if the search is made with your consent you should signify that fact by signing a Notice of Powers and Rights. If not with your consent, you must be informed of the purpose and grounds of the search. With regard to demanding a right of entry into your home for the purposes of searching it, not associated with arrest, the police officer may obtain a search warrant from a magistrate under s 8 of the

PACE 1984. We have already noted from *Rice v Connolly* (1966) that any attempt to obstruct the above searches will be an offence under s 51(3) of the Police Act 1964.

Detention

Upon an arrest a person is taken to be detained at a police station. Section 37(2) of the PACE 1984 makes clear that the purpose of such a detention is to secure a confession. This detention period can be up to 24 hours, increasing to 96 hours for a serious arrestable offence (or up to seven days under the Prevention of Terrorism (Temporary Provisions) Act 1989). Once in detention at the police station any police interviews should be conducted in accordance with Codes C and E. The significant safeguards here are that a suspect should be cautioned, a contemporaneous recording/tape recording made of the interview with an opportunity for the person interviewed to read over and sign the record of the interview, the notification and right to legal advice and, where appropriate, the presence of an adult.

Police impropriety

It is apparent from the aforementioned that the police enjoy considerable powers to restrict your personal liberty. Such extensive powers, we are told, are necessary to facilitate the effective policing of our State. Thus our constitutional safeguards as potential suspects lie not in the restriction of the scope of the powers but more in the supervision of the 'reasonable' exercise of these powers. But what penalty awaits the law enforcement officer who acts unreasonably in the exercise of his or her power?

Exclusion of evidence

In addition to any writ of *habeas corpus* or claims to self defence which may be applicable, the first redress one may have for police impropriety could be the refusal of the judge to allow evidence to be used. If a confession has been extracted by a police officer using oppressive tactics, it can be excluded by the judge under s 76(2)a of the PACE 1984. Indeed, the example of the 'Cardiff Three' demonstrates the power of judges in the Court of Appeal to quash convictions due to oppressive questioning. If in other ways a confession has been extracted in circumstances conducive of unreliability the judge may exclude it under s 76(2)b of the PACE 1984. The judge also has a power to exclude a confession if admitting it might create unfairness at the trial. Section 78 of the PACE 1984 allows for the exclusion of physical evidence if the police officer obtained the evidence with deliberate illegality. We should note that whatever its limited practical effect, s 82 of the PACE 1984 still retains a discretion for the judge under common law to exclude evidence.

Damages

A second redress may be to institute a claim for damages against the police. This approach is limited by the fact that breaches of Codes, Notes for Guidance and Home Office Circulars do not give rise to liability. Moreover, it would appear that some of the statutory provisions of PACE, such as s 58 and the entitlement to legal advice, are also treated by judges in a similar fashion. (For the common law rules which preceded the Act and have not been abrogated by it see *R v Chief Constable of South Wales, ex p Merrick* (1994).)

However, the breach of statutory arrest or detention rules may give grounds to a claim for damages for false imprisonment. The excessive use of force by a police officer may lead to a claim for damages for assault and battery and a right to prosecute the police officer. Trespass to land or to goods may occur if a police officer fails to follow the statutory rules relating to search and seizure. Finally, a tort action for malicious prosecution will be available if the police have abused their powers in recommending prosecution.

Formal compliant

The third method by which one may seek a redress for police impropriety is to institute a formal complaint against the police officer with the police themselves. Here the police officer may be internally disciplined for breaches of the Codes. However, it is generally agreed that this complaints procedure (with the supervision of the Police Complaints Authority in allegations of serious misconduct) lacks the trust of both the general public and the police themselves as an effective means of redressing a grievance.

Further public disquiet with the criminal justice system in the wake of the more recent miscarriages of justice (Guildford Four, Birmingham Six, etc) led to the setting up a Royal Commission on Criminal Justice in 1993 under the chairmanship of Lord Runciman. However, a number of the findings of the Commission have been rejected by the government. In particular, ss 34–37 of the Criminal Justice and Public Order Act 1994 now curtails a suspect's rights to silence in that an inference may now be drawn from a suspect's silence at his or her trial.

(We should also note the work of a new Criminal Justice Commission, which since the early part of 1997 has taken over responsibility from the Home Office for the consideration of possible miscarriages of justice.)

Tipping the balance with issues of national security

We have already seen that issues of national security permeate a wide range of areas. In the employment field we saw in *Council for Civil Service Unions v Minister for the Civil Service* (1985) the use of national security to defeat a legal challenge to the banning of trade unions at GCHQ. In the study of our freedom of association and assembly we noted common law offences and the effect of public order legislation. The case of *Malone v Metropolitan Police Commissioner* (1979) raised the issue of State interception of communications and prompted the passing of the Interception of Communications Act 1985. The regulation of electronic and other surveillance techniques is undertaken by s 3 of the Intelligence Services Act 1994.

Deportation orders have also been served in the interest of national security. In *R v Home Secretary, ex p Hosenball* (1977) a deportation order was made against an American journalist who proposed publishing an article about how our government monitored communications. *R v Home Secretary, ex p Cheblak* (1991) saw a deportation order made, during the Gulf hostilities, against a person who had lived in this country since 1975. In both instances the government refused to furnish further information to the court justifying their decisions again on the grounds of national security.

The *Prevention of Terrorism Bill* was passed in 24 hours and within eight days of the Birmingham pub bombings in November 1974, without virtual amendment or dissent. This legislation was the forerunner to the present Prevention of Terrorism (Temporary Provisions) Act 1989. Notices censoring the broadcasting of certain political views from Northern Ireland have been made, in the interests of national security, under the Broadcasting Act 1981 (see *R v Home Secretary, ex p Brind* (1991)).

In *R v Secretary of State for the Home Department, ex p Gallagher* (1995), the European Court of Justice was required by the Court of Appeal to consider the procedure employed under the Prevention of Terrorism (Temporary Provisions) Act 1989 for the making of exclusion orders.

The court ruled that, save in cases of urgency, no exclusion order should be made without the opinion first being sought by a competent authority with 'independent status' from the decision-maker.

Current interest is focusing on national security considerations inherent in the Prevention of Terrorism (Additional Powers) Act 1996. This Act completed its passage through both Houses of Parliament in just two days, and granted the police extensive powers to stop and search pedestrians, impose cordons, prohibit passing, search non-residential premises and unaccompanied goods.

Official secrets

Yet nowhere is the UK attitude to national security better illustrated than in the degree of balance which is allowed to exist between an individual's access to information and the need for State secrecy. Information is often said to be the currency of power and there is much within our constitution that limits your freedom to information on the governing of your State. Indeed, the Official Secrets Acts 1911 and 1989 and the Public Records Act 1967 have as their primary purpose the restriction of your access to State sensitive information.

The Official Secrets Act 1911 was hurriedly passed by Parliament in response to a general fear about spying. The case of *Chandler v DPP* (1964) demonstrated, however, the wide terms used in the Act when it was held to cover a CND demonstration at a US military air base in this country. After continued public disquiet the Franks Committee in 1972 recommended repeal of the Act because of its unacceptably wide drafting and 'catch-all' provisions. It was not until *R v Ponting* (1985) and his acquittal by the jury for leaking information to Parliament about the sinking of the *General Belgrano*, however, that the government accepted the need to reform the Act.

The new Official Secrets Act 1989 divides the protected information into specific categories:

- security and intelligence (s 1);
- defence (s 2);
- international relations (s 3);
- criminal investigations (s 4).

The Act requires that the leak of information needs to be a 'damaging' disclosure in order to initiate a prosecution. Certain defences are also permitted, but not the defence of 'public interest' as raised by Clive Ponting.

Spycatcher

In addition to these restrictions placed on the access to information under the criminal law, the civil law also allows for restriction under breach of confidence. Breach of confidence is now given statutory recognition in s 5 of the Official Secrets Act 1989. Instances of its operation would include *A-G v Jonathan Cape* (1976) and litigation associated with the book, *Spycatcher*. The *Spycatcher* litigation commenced in Australia, where Peter Wright was resident and first intended publishing his book. The government attempted to restrain publication on the basis that the secrets contained within the book were acquired by Wright as part of his contract of employment and therefore he was selling them in breach of confidence. The book contained allegations of a conspiracy amongst members of MI5 to 'destabilise' the Wilson administration of the 1970s, a previous head of the UK intelligence service was a Soviet spy, a plot to assassinate President Nasser of Egypt and numerous illegal burglaries carried out against members of CND.

When the *Observer* and *Guardian* newspapers published articles on the impending trial, the Attorney-General secured an interim injunction against publication of information obtained by Wright as an MI5 officer. When the government lost at trial in March 1987 they secured undertakings not to publish pending an appeal. But in April the *Independent, Evening News* and *London Daily News* wrote articles about the book and were made subject to contempt proceedings. In July *The Sunday Times* published extracts of the book, which was about to be published in the USA, and the Attorney-General secured an interlocutory injunction against further publications. Judges in the House of Lords then reaffirmed all the interlocutory injunctions in *A-G v Guardian Newspapers* (1987).

In September the government lost its appeal to the New South Wales Court of Appeal which refused to restrain further publication pending a further appeal to the High Court of Australia (this court dismissed the government's action in June 1989). In the following year the government failed in its attempt to convince Judges in the House of Lords of the merits of a permanent injunction. Given the book's world-wide publication Lord Keith took the view that, 'such secrets as the book may contain have been revealed to any intelligence service whose interests are opposed to those of the United Kingdom'. In a sense this demonstrated a refreshing willingness on the part of our Judges to question for themselves the interests which are at stake.

However, our press were less than happy with the outcome of the litigation and took the matter to the European Commission on Human

Rights. In *Observer v UK* (1991) the Court held that the failure of the House of Lords to discharge the injunctions in 1987, when the book was already available in the USA, violated Article 10 of the European Convention on Human Rights.

In this regard it is interesting to note that in *Attorney-General v Blake* (1996) Sir Richard Scott VC ruled that the Crown was not entitled to the profits gained by Blake, a former Secret Intelligence Officer who became a Soviet Agent in 1951, for when his autobiography was published in 1989 none of the information was any longer confidential. To grant relief would, it was therefore felt, entail an infringement of Blake's rights under Article 10 of the European Convention.

Freedom of Information Act?

Our right of access to personal files is limited to the Data Protection Act 1984 (which under an EC Directive is soon to be extended to paper records); the Access to Personal Files Act 1987; the Access to Medical Reports Act 1988 and the Access to Health Records Act 1990. Our right of access to general information is largely limited to the Local Government (Access to Information) Act 1985. But does this lack of access to information and consequent secrecy necessarily lead to a better administered State?

When campaigning for his Private Members 'Right to Know' Bill 1993, Mark Fisher MP argued that secret decisions are more likely to be bad decisions and thus a greater openness would inevitably improve the quality of decisions.

In particular, it was noted that in 1985 more than 50 people died in a fire at the Bradford City Football Club. Confidential correspondence from the local council a few months earlier had complained about the 'unacceptable' fire hazard. In 1987 31 people died in a fire at Kings Cross underground station. Again confidential warnings had previously been given. In the *Marchioness* river boat tragedy of 1989 confidential accident reports hid from the public the fact that the *Bowbelle*, the vessel which had crashed into the *Marchioness*, had a history of previous river accidents. The point made is that whereas nobody knows whether these tragedies could have been avoided by greater openness it is possible that a greater public awareness of the problems may have had an effect and little was served by keeping the information secret.

But even States with a Freedom of Information Act recognise that some information relating to the operation of their State needs to be kept secret. In Australia, for example, 74% of requests for information in 1990–91 were granted in full, but 22% had some information withheld and the remaining 4% of requests were denied altogether. Thus the position adopted by government to date is to maintain the existing approach but to seek to promote greater openness within it.

To this end the 1993 White Paper, 'Open Government' aims to 'identify areas of excessive secrecy in government and to propose ways of increasing openness'. In this spirit of openness, Premier Major offered an insight into the structure of Cabinet government and its Committees. The security services have also been put on a legal footing under the Security Services Act 1989 and the Intelligence Services Act 1994 and have given us an indication of their present priorities. A Code of Practice has also been created on Access to Government Information.

Yet if all this represents a step in the right direction, then it has to be said that it is only a very limited step. In the view of Professor Richard Stone, 'so far, the government's commitment to greater openness has not been matched with any convincing progress in that direction'. Reviewing the operation of the new Code of Practice in March 1996, the Select Committee on the Parliamentary Commissioner for Administration concluded that there should now be a single Freedom of Information Act encompassing all access rights to government information. This reform would, in the view of the Committee, provide for greater accuracy and objectivity of personal files; improve decision-making by Ministers and civil servants; inform public debate on issues of the day and ultimately help the government to appreciate the commercial value of the information it holds about us.

Time for a Bill of Rights?

Concern for the protection of individual freedoms within our State centre upon the fact that Diceyan assurances of civil liberties within our constitution relate to a State that has since undergone radical change. Lord Bingham, warned us in 1993 that:

> ... constitutional organs, like constellations, wax and wane and change position relative to each other and the present century has seen such changes in our constitutional arrangements. Most striking has been the increase in the size and power of the executive, in particular the Prime Minister, the Cabinet and Ministers. Almost equally striking has been the weakening of parliamentary influence on the conduct of governments. For this there are no doubt many explanations, but the decline of the independent Member,

the doctrine of the electoral mandate, the tightening of party discipline and the less deferential attitude of constituency parties are probably among them. At the same time Parliament, in practice if not in theory, has ceded a part of its sovereignty: for the first time ever a secular body beyond the mountains can bindingly declare Acts of Parliament to be unlawful. And the increase of executive power has been matched by a degree of judicial review unthinkable even a few years ago. Where does all this leave the protection of human rights?

The answer, according to people like Lord Scarman, is that the aforementioned leaves our modern multi-racial State in need of a new Bill of Rights. It is not needed this time to protect the interests of Parliament against the Crown, but rather to uphold the concept of the rule of law by giving legal protection to our interests as individual citizens of the State. But if the UK were to have a new Bill of Rights then questions would inevitably arise as to what rights should be included, whether it should and could be entrenched, who would enforce it and how would it be enforced?

ECHR

With a membership in 1993 of 32 States, the Council of Europe was formed in 1949 in the aftermath of the Second World War and the Nuremberg Trials. It has as its aims furthering the ideals of political democracy and the protection of fundamental human rights. To this end the original members formulated a European Convention on Human Rights to which to the UK was one of the original signatories in 1950. Lord Bingham notes that contained within the Convention and its subsequent Protocols are the following positive rights (subject to qualifications) which were drafted in the main part by UK lawyers:

> ... the right to life; the right to protection against subjection to torture or inhuman or degrading treatment or punishment; the prohibition of slavery and forced labour; the liberty and security of the person; the right to a fair trial; the prohibition of retrospective criminal legislation; the right to respect for private and family life, home and correspondence; the right to freedom of thought, conscience and religion; the right to freedom of expression; the right to freedom of peaceful assembly and association; the right to marry and found a family; the right to peaceful enjoyment of property; the right to education; the requirement that there be free elections at reasonable intervals by secret ballot; and the right to enjoy these rights and freedoms without discrimination on any ground.

To effect the enforcement of these rights the Council of Europe established both a European Commission on Human Rights and a European Court of Human Rights. The number of cases before the court has increased dramatically, from 404 in 1981 to 1,861 in 1992. In order to facilitate proceedings, these two bodies, the Commission and the ECHR, are to be united.

Article 24 allows for one Member State (High Contracting Party) to bring an action against another State for breaches of the ECHR (such as Eire did against the UK in 1971 and 1972 in respect of the activities of the security forces in Northern Ireland). Article 25 provides for a right of individual petition for breaches of the ECHR. If there was opposition within the UK to the idea of signing the ECHR, such as Lord Chancellor Jowitt who did not want, 'to jeopardise our whole system of law ... in favour of some half-baked scheme to be administered by some unknown court', then there was outright hostility to the idea of its application via individual petition. This hostility continued up to 1966 when the decision was taken to allow for a limited period the right of individual petition to the Commission. Such applications can only be made within six months from the date when all domestic challenges are exhausted (Article 26). It is at this stage that the Commission 'filters out' the 90% or more of 'inadmissible' applications under Article 27. The remaining 10% or so are investigated by the Commission which, under Article 28, attempts to effect a 'friendly settlement'. If no solution is reached then the matter is referred to the Committee of Ministers and the European Court of Human Rights.

But whereas our State has signed the European Convention on Human Rights and now allows for a right of individual petition for alleged breaches of it, the Convention has not been incorporated into our domestic law. This has led to an intensive debate on the weight our Judges should accord to the rights upheld within the Convention (see the works of Professor Jowell and 'Fundamental Rights: The United Kingdom Isolated? Anthony Lester QC (1984) *Public Law*). In *R v Chief Immigration Officer, Heathrow Airport, ex p Salamat Bibi* (1976), Lord Denning retreated from his earlier statement in *R v Home Secretary, ex p Bhajan Singh* (1976) and held that it would be asking too much for immigration officers, 'to know or to apply the Convention ... much better for us to stick to our own statutes and principles, and only look to the Convention for guidance in case of doubt'.

This interpretative 'gap-filler' role for the ECHR hit problems, however, in *Malone v Metropolitan Police Commissioner* (1979), where there was not so much a gap as a gaping hole which needed to be filled. The situation forced *Sir Robert Megarry V-C* to conclude that whereas he would:

> ... readily seek to construe ... legislation in a way which would effectuate the Convention rather than frustrate it ... It seems to me that where Parliament has abstained from legislating on a point that is plainly suitable for legislation, it is indeed difficult ... to lay down new rules of common law or equity.

(Note the subsequent passing of the Interception of Communications Act 1985.)

A similar approach was offered by Lord Bridge in the case of *R v Home Secretary, ex p Brind* (1991) when he drew a clear line between the mere resolution of any ambiguity and enforced conformity with the ECHR. Lord Bridge and his fellow Judges in the House of Lords could find no ambiguity in s 29(3) of the Broadcasting Act 1981, under which power the relevant Notice had been issued.

One of the more recent decisions in this area has been *Derbyshire CC v Times Newspapers* (1993). Balcombe LJ in the Court of Appeal, noting Lord Goff's assessment in *A-G v Guardian Newspapers (No 2)* (1990) that there was no difference in principle between our freedom of speech and Article 10 of the ECHR, placed great weight on the Convention which in his view was useful to resolve ambiguities in both legislation and the common law and could guide Judges in applying their discretion, eg interlocutory relief. Judges in the House of Lords, and Lord Keith in particular, reaffirmed the decision of the Court of Appeal but saw little need to use the ECHR when the matter was already adequately covered by domestic law.

However, Professor Richard Stone in his book *Civil Liberties* (1994) concludes that:

> ... we may perhaps expect that 'the language of Strasbourg' ... will gradually, but ever more frequently, become accepted as part of English jurisprudence, and that the ECHR and the common law will continue to converge, even without the formal adoption of the Convention into English law.

Others would argue that the ECHR is already undergoing a process of indirect adoption. There may be two distinct bodies operating within Europe, with the European Union (though in strict terms ECSC; EURATOM and the European Community remain as distinct communities) and the Council of Europe, but this is not to say that their work does not overlap. Both recently looked at the ban in Eire on disseminating information about abortion services (unlawful under the Irish

Constitution) in the UK. The European Court of Justice looked at the issue from the perspective of free trade and the European Court of Human Rights from the perspective of Article 10 and the right to receive and impart information.

Although the European Court of Justice has recently ruled that there is no current provision within the Treaties for accession by the Community to the Convention, Lord Slynn would point out that:

> ... every time the European Court recognises a principle set out in the Convention as being part of Community law, it must be enforced in the United Kingdom courts in relation to Community law matters, but not in domestic law. So the Convention becomes in part a part of our law through the back door.

Evidence for this development can be seen in Lord Browne-Wilkinson's article, 'The Infiltration of a Bill of Rights' (1992) *Public Law.*

For many commentators problems of entrenchment and enforcement can be overcome and it would be better if the ECHR were now to enter by the front door. In his article, 'The European Convention on Human Rights: Time to Incorporate' (1993) *Law Quarterly Review*, Lord Bingham emotively asserts:

> ... that the ability of English Judges to protect human rights in this country and reconcile conflicting rights ... is inhibited by the failure of successive governments over many years to incorporate into United Kingdom law the European Convention on Human Rights.

We should heed the words of Reinhold Niebuhr when he states that:

> it is man's capacity for justice that makes democracy possible; it is man's inclination to injustice that makes democracy necessary.

Perhaps the time has now come to assert a democratic claim to the fundamental human rights protected within the Convention?

Index